I0242286

FINISHING LINE PRESS
www.finishinglinepress.com

AND
&
AND

poems by

Bob King

Finishing Line Press
Georgetown, Kentucky

AND
&
AND

For Bridget

ISBN 979-8-88838-686-6 First Edition

Publisher: Leah Huete de Maines
Editor: Christen Kincaid
Cover Art: "Sultry Cleveland Light" by Megan Frankenfield
Author Photo: Bridget C. King
Cover Design: Elizabeth Maines McCleavy

Order online: www.finishinglinepress.com
also available on amazon.com

Author inquiries and mail orders:
Finishing Line Press
PO Box 1626
Georgetown, Kentucky 40324
USA

Contents

I.

Part of a Traveling Exhibition

What if there really are hidden portals
that transport us to another dimension
& of course we can't see the possible
half-dozen exits—like sides of dice—
unique to each of us because Steve Jobs
hadn't yet invented the device that when
held in front of our faces reveals our potential
chalk outlines shimmering like brightly-lit
Pokémon appearing from virtual mist. But
they're there, these world-scattered portals
perhaps disguised as potholes or memory-
foam-mattress body indentations, & when
we gamble & hit one of our six just right—
with door-to-cabinet frame, metal-to-magnet
silvery click precision—click-boom we're
gone gone gone, leaving behind family
& six friends to place what's left among
the dogwood-root tendrils & flaky pieces
of freshly displaced soil. Like that poor kid
from River who passed just a couple weeks ago,
fallen from an ATV on a Lake Erie island, a world
away from his Australian childhood. He couldn't
have known that his portal would be a perfect
beach-road click-match & his buddies would
have to walk away carrying the terrible gravity
of knowing it wasn't their door. Their threshold.
Their time. Or the time my grandfather must've
unconsciously twitch-clicked just precisely in
his den's hospice bed, his mutant esophagus
cells finally sealing shut that corporeal tunnel,
& from the living room Liz, Tom, & I heard
the vacuum whoosh of his final breath,
like an air-lock chamber before he clunky-
spacesuit lumbered out into the starlit
void. Or like those double-door glass

passageways that lead from the exotic
butterfly enclosure back into the broader zoo,
the burst of wind ensuring you don't have
a dainty turquoise hitchhiker in your hair,
on your shoulder, its wings just barely
moving—you'll have to squint or don a pair
of readers to notice the flutter, yet should
your butterfly—your transformed wizard
of science & magic—escape to that vaster
universe, it'd only take a slight perspective
shift to realize his new world isn't a danger
to him. It doesn't mean he's gone or lost.
But he's off to possibility & adventure,
as he'll smell cotton candy for the first
time, drink from a sunny-spotted garden
of brightly-hued asters, drift over mesmerizing
splashing waters of synchronized fountains,
& soar among the treetops, grateful that
something like the majesty of giraffes
can even exist.

Briquette

There is this person, or, there are those people in the backyard & for some odd reason, in the most unlikely situations, I come to love them. They're energizing & repulsive. They pulsate gratification. They fill that space, always that space, between myself & others, or myself & the vegetable tray. Then I think about how the best way to do it is blindfolded. How the truth is always urgently vulgar—how I burn my food & eat it & spit it out, & then burn it again & eat it & spit it out. I've ruined my best shirt doing this. It's not an emergency. It's just, I don't like leftovers. And I'd rather someone scantily clad than not clad at all. I like a little difficulty. There may be easier, healthier ways of proceeding, but simplicity can't invoke excitement again & again & again. This is not to say don't be familiar—just don't be routine. It's to stress the importance of surprise, of complication, of you being able to tell me, "You're wrong. You're being an asshole." It's not about passion completely. It's about you looking great in a dress & even better in overalls.

The Birds Know Why

The birds know why my wife sleep-talk-
mumbled when I got into bed an hour
after her, & apparently only the birds
know why. The birds don't know why
the English call their women birds, but
apparently Mary the Virgin was called
a *burde* with a *U* & an *E* & as the spelling
changed, it stuck & the birds know
why. Or perhaps they're jailbirds,
caged & singing, as when we *do bird,*
slang for *doing time*, & only the birds
know why & it's not too different
from Americans & *chicks* & yeah yeah,
can you dig it, you jazz saxophonist,
you Charlie Parker migrating your
notes all over Manhattan where &
when even the birds on the wires were
calling out our names like counted crows
& entertained & improvised & no longer
empty-staffed empty-noted sheet music.
Longing is both the cause & effect of
belonging. *My wife whose rump is sandstone*
& flax / whose rump is the back of a swan
& the spring / my wife with the sex
of an iris / a mine and a platypus
& call enough women birds & soon
enough, you become the migrator,
you become the lonely traveler,
as lonely as a traveler in the American
West in a Cormac McCarthy novel,
which isn't too different from loneliness
in a Hopper painting, which isn't too
different from the French & their love
of alienation & existentialism, which isn't
too different from both the myth itself
& the destruction of the myth of
the American Dream, family unit,
masculinity or loneliness itself in
Willy's death in *Death of a Salesman* or
disintegration in a Sam Shepard play.
Like a Northern Cardinal sitting alone
in a berry-barren crabapple tree during
mid-December's first snowstorm. Do

the birds know why there's burnt toast
& corn husks all over the stage? Are
those same birds picky about the hybrid
crops they eat, particularly in the loneliness
of the season's first snowstorm? Why some
birds can understand each other's
separate language, while others can't.
I'd love to speak French or Hindi, but
I'm a sadly single-tooled westerner.
Why some birds build & use multipart
tools & Homo sapiens can't until our
5th birthday. Why migration, why brood
parasites or infanticide. Pebble exchange
& nests from fishing line & cigarette
butts. Why with that brain as big as
a grain of rice they can recognize human
faces, grasp self, act like Machiavelli,
display their façade memory like humans
& like humans give taxonomy to species'
feces, roll with monogamy or promiscuity
or corkscrew-shaped genitalia, & sort
those elaborate New Guinean jungle
courtship rituals, dressed in their most
glitzy & bedazzled Broadway costumes.
My wife whose hair is a brush fire
whose thoughts are summer lightning
my wife knows why Australian hawks
track brush fires & have even been known
to fly with lit sticks to drop & arson another
patch of scrub, shrubbery, undergrowth.
The birds know why. The birds know.
They know why curiosity—my wife's
most noble characteristic. *My wife with*
eyes that are forests forever under the axe
my wife with eyes that are the equal
of water and air and earth and fire.
And the Bowerbird asks, Are the blue
decorations enough for you? Are my
cognitive abilities capable enough,
to the point where you'd sleep
with me? You do know you're the
architect of my neural networks &
artistic creations, beauty evolved from
your perception of beauty, my survival
always mostly a matter of mostly your

aesthetics. Mini delicious flying dinosaurs,
I think I'd rather fight 1 10-foot chicken
than 100 1-foot white domesticated fowl
beside the red wheelbarrow glazed
with rainwater. Orioles & Cardinals
& Blue Jays & Sesame Street's giant
anthropomorphic bird who frequently
misunderstands the why of the why,
& it's not an albatross if you go to
therapy to learn to see things differently,
which is one of the main differences
between adult & juvenile feather
patterns. The fact is, the birds know
why if/when I have trouble sleeping,
if/why my brain's on fire & need to
reset my hair on fire, all I have to do
is press my bare chest, my birdcage,
my ribcage to the back of my wife's
ribcage, beats synchronizing like
jazz, like the release of something
terrible, just by naming it, just by
saying it & singing it & maybe even
loving it & the birds know why.

Upon Seeing a Red-Headed Ground Beetle I've Decided: I'm More About *Protection of the Weak* Than I Am *Survival of the Fittest*

Look, most of what we do, directly or indirectly,
is about distracting us from the fact that
we'll all be dead soon. We're all just renters.
But maybe it's also about being remembered
after we're kaput. Squished. Entombed. See also:
headstones & mausoleums, which really
are just fancy Post-it Notes for the future
generations for when they walk through
the field-cemetery-kitchen of our past lives:
we hope they see the hasty scribble & forgive
us for eating all the plums in the icebox which
they were probably saving but were so delicious
& sweet & we simply couldn't help
ourselves. Don't be a plum eater. Think of
others. Conserve. Learn trivia along the trail:
Did you know Darwin's Galopagoan boat
was called the *Beetle?* Wait. That's not true.
It was the *Beagle*. But I misheard the podcast
or the lyrics & thought John, Paul, & George
might've been trying to make some kind of evolved
statement after the hard days & nights in Hamburg,
where their 10,000 hours of play transformed them
from amateurs into experts. But no. They weren't
naturalists or activists. Yet. Did you know that
Neanderthals were most likely gingers—red tufted
& freckled & soulless & Germanic with limited
language but urgent with their *hubba hubba* eyebrow
arches in their pastoral pickup joints because
procreation. Because without procreation they
knew that the Homo sapiens on their way from
Africa would try to exterminate or assimilate or both.
Most of us still have at least 2% Neanderthal DNA.
That's a fact, you post-extinction caveman. Red yarn
red yarn red yarn—butterfly effect—& like an amateur
detective I can red yarn from Ethiopia to Hamburg
to the Cuyahoga Valley National Park & red yarn
from my footfalls on the crushed limestone towpath
to a quick scamper off-route & after taking a leak
beside a walnut tree like my epically aged ancestors,
like an expert I bend to check out the Red-Headed
Ground Beetle feasting on aphids just outside
Szalay's sweet corn field. Yes, it's true that this

ginger beetle is capable of mixing chemicals
in her dual pygidial glands—her butt—yes, in
her marvelous ass she can blend fluid & create
a combustion engine & POP! hot acrid gas
ejects & is capable of paralyzing even a small
mammal, like a shrew, which is why some beetles
are called bombardier beetles & even Darwin
got bombed by one, but that's not what took him
out. No. He was run over by a Volkswagen Bug
in the ironies to end ironies because like Alanis
Morissette, it's not ironic. And it's not true.
The Bug wasn't invented until about 50 years
after Darwin's ticker stopped, & even
the combined idea & design of Ferdinand
Porsche & Adolph Hitler couldn't have
resurrected a father of evolution, which—
red yarn—can be easily corrupted,
like anything, because as good as we are
at discovery & invention, our penchant
for perversion & exploitation of a good idea
is just as strong. See evolution. See eugenics.
See entomology. See deforestation. See politics.
See coup d'état. But the truth also is that Red-
Headed Beetles are beneficial creatures, despite
their incredible capacity for cruelty. Cruelty
isn't the point. For them. For us. Even the smallest
creatures make the globe spin like good vinyl.
And when all the broken-hearted people—broken
by the bullies & belligerent coaches & teachers
& family members & cliquey kids in a field
with a weaponized magnifying glass—yes,
*when all the broken-hearted people living in
the world agree*—agree that there's more power
in being a cheerleader than there is being a critic—
there will be an answer. Yes, there will be an answer.

At What Point Does a Superpower Become a Burden?

For Isabelle

By how much would your life improve
if you could see the thought bubbles
we all carry like tethered amoeba above
our heads? As if you're trying to take
a photo in the distance, you hold up your
phone, & the guy blocking the whole
damn cereal aisle with his cart comes
into focus. Tap. "A three-dollar difference
is the difference in making it to the next
check. They'll get used to generic."
And so, you wait. Until next time,
when you're at the soccer field,
& you play like you're zooming-in
to better see the scoreboard, spotting
your daughter racing up the right wing
with a (tap) pulsing ball of, "If I score,
I'll make him proud," & then slyly
focus on the puffy-eyed lady wearing
the puffy jacket who hasn't stopped
coughing since kickoff, & you wonder:
with the right filter, will you be able to see
the brand of virus particles in her bubble,
slowly leaking air, gradually tangling with
others' kites. You turn & turn. His looks
like a concrete-filled beanbag, folding over
his forehead, slumping over his shoulders,
anchoring his eyes to the ground. Theirs
twist & rustle & tumble like plastic
grocery bags among the cars in a vast
parking lot. And finally, you lock eyes
with a little old lady in a matted fur coat.
She smiles at you. Reaches up. Gathers
several dark strings from above the fans
crowded around her. She extends her hand.
Those anvil clouds quickly time-lapse into
multicolored tear-drops, swollen with
helium, "It's not so bad," she says,
"once you learn to let them go."

Sometimes I Worry That My Imposter Syndrome Isn't Good Enough Imposter Syndrome

There was a period of several months
where Tchaikovsky thought his head
would spontaneously detach from his
neck while he was conducting, so he took
to holding onto his chin his beard with his
left hand while he worked the baton with
his right. Final bow, final bow, *The Nutcracker
Suite*. The opium poppy was once used
to treat addiction itself, but once it was
realized that opium itself was addictive
they went & derived morphine from
the same plant to treat that addiction,
& once they realized that morphine
was addictive too, they went & derived
heroin from the same plant to treat
the morphine-slash-opium addiction.
How long are you going to do the same
thing & expect a different result? How
we conduct ourselves when no one
is watching is character. How others
perceive us while we conduct is called
reputation. Sometimes we need to get
out of our own way & try to forget
the audience, even as we try to merge
into civilized society, & realize most
are not, in fact, civilized, & are making
it up as they go along, tornados rooted
to a spot with a few recurring central
images: old Ford pickup, mooing cow,
lady on a bicycle swirling around us,
& even if the wind never dies down,
it's still a weirdly worthwhile life.

A Review of *History of the Rain* by Niall Williams

Not knowing has never stopped anyone
from creating a narrative in which they
pretend to know. You can sleep soundly
now that you've given yourself an acceptable
explanation. For most, randomness is not
enough. After all, people still cling to
the random morality of their conquerors,
even when it conflicts with what they know
in their gut to be true & for most, truth can't
be random. Or nuanced. Either it's raining
or it's not. A little bit of truth doesn't have
the same charm as a little bit of fog while
sipping hot tea. Time has the power to
turn heartbreak into a fairytale & fairytale
into the textbook history of how a nation
was stripped or founded, a butcher's apron
& blighted drills the final overcome excuses
to participate in a great migration. But even
if our ancestors fled those once-trod fields,
those facts give us no claim to one speck
of said soil now. A little bit of identity
just doesn't have the same charm as
the whole truth & any claim otherwise
should be proof enough to earn derision
even if derision was borne of a shaky
hypothesis. Bridget, being adored
makes you adorable, even if the used
prepositions are *to, from,* & *by* me.
The world looks joyful to the joyful,
miserable to the miserable, & I still
believe that we still count, that together
we count, that our counting will be worth
something, even if it's only belief. In '98
we looked out from the craggy North Atlantic
shore of Achill Island, your father's roots,
the rarity of a full week's stay without
a drop of rain, & speaking of your ancestors
you said, *Now I understand why they left.*
We agreed then & there we'd sacrifice
for our daughters, our future hypothetical
granddaughters, but what about their
granddaughters & theirs & theirs & theirs?
Who has that much foresight? That much

compassion? Did they? Did ours? Where's
the line in the distance, future or past,
where we can safely not care about our
ancestors or progeny? Who has that much
insight? And yet when you allow wonder,
you will see wonder, just as when you
practice avoidance, you sometimes avoid
those things you'd be better off experiencing.
When your dream legs are longer than your
real ones, you keep running, trying desperately
to catch up, running through spiderwebs
spread across the trail—filaments disguised
as finish lines—& spiderwebs are what
the invisible would look like if it was visible,
beauty & truth disguised as you or you
as them, & the compassionate rarely
receive in return the compassion they
put out into the world. We are not living
inside a James Joyce novel, we are not art
for art's sake, nor are we obscene because
the definition of *obscene* changes depending
on the reader or institution & who are they
to judge our obscenity when they ignore
& forgive the very obscenities they work
so hard to preach against? We choose
our moral outrages. They all do. But
we're not *Do as I say & not as I do.* We
are not yet a moment of Yeatsian uplift,
we are not McCourt's ashes from ashes,
nor O'Brien's O'Brienness, but we do relate
to Heaney's digging. Those you turn to
in moments of emergency often have
no one to turn to in their own moments.
Check up on your friends. And I didn't
fully realize in the moment that I decided
to see the world as marvelous that I'd
never lose my ability to marvel.

Meme Machine: /*noun*/ Nothing More Than Cogs & Gears That Produce Cultural Replications, Fanciful Flights, & Losing Battles for Long-Term Evolution, Unless You End Up Under Glass in the Natural History Museum

Hey Holden, there's more to a cliff
than its edge. There's an entire field
of kids running around behind you
that you could be running with,
remembering what it's like to stay
in the moment. So here, young man,
take off that bulky overcoat & silly hat
& spread them near the edge & watch
the sun slowly descend over the distant
hills, the starling murmuration morphing,
your anxious brain for once quieted
by that fluid mobius strip of birds,
symbolism exploding before your eyes:
they're a sheep flock now a gently flowing
river now a lion charging across the cloudless
savanna of the sky after an antelope, & now
a metaphor of a metaphor of a metaphor.
High functioning anxious people are
the type of people you want around
in an emergency, even if anxiousness
is hard to live with in nonemergency
situations. Which are most situations.
The quietness evasive. Like happiness
in a Chekhov play. You see, most of life
is a battle between your genes' battle
to be selfish & self-replicating, to ensure
their own survival, & those same genes
weighing how much they need to cooperate,
as if state-required auto insurance,
or a *C's-get-degrees* student—*What's*
the bare minimum I need to do to get by?—
for if your genes don't work in concert,
then they are nothing more than
a lonely cello playing in an otherwise
empty & drafty barn, a fallow field
visible through the rotted planks,
the lack of radiance not dissimilar
to a Chekhov play. Our brains still
possess an incredible capacity: they
can observe, orient, decide, & act
in .4 seconds, which means in one

second, we can observe, orient, decide,
& act 2.5 times. My Corolla now spinning
on the ice on I-77 North &, Oh look,
there's a Northern Cardinal asleep
on a dark pine trunk, its head-bob-
fighting-to-stay-awake barely perceptible
through the again-snow-flurries, not
unlike a butterfly in a James Wright
poem, & in these cold distances
of the afternoon that JESUS SAVES
billboard is new, & now, 180-degrees
from the direction I should be pointed
is the tractor-trailer that's going to end
me, & all the while my foot is going
from the gas to the brake & back, hands
are turning into it or out of it—I forget
which is which but thank god for the
thick-foil-wrapped Honey Baked Ham
perched on my neck possessing some
kind of muscle memory, allowing my
hand-over-hand clockworking around
the steering wheel, reacting before
my consciousness is even conscious
of action. BTW, that's the OODA Loop,
that .4 second cycle of observe, orient,
decide, & act, & loop loop loop.
Oh, believe me I know: we're not always
interested in knowing how things work,
until things don't work, & then we only
want an explanation as to why it broke,
but then we usually just want it fixed
without getting into the nitty-gritty,
save the cost. Did you expect emotional
repair to be affordable? If we unpack all
our body's cellular membranes & lay them
flat, they'd cover the area of 151 football
fields. That's almost 750 blue whales—
Hey, I speak whale. Lemme try humpback—
or 900,000 large-sized-but-flattened
Amazon boxes, or almost 8 million
uncrumpled & unwaxy Taco Bell taco
wrappers. With extra Fire sauce. Always
bring the heat. We belch in the general
direction of the metric system. Proof
we'll never stop fighting the bloody

Redcoats. When really confused &
we're sure no one's looking, we still
sometimes count on our fingers.
There was one sperm. One egg.
One just-healthy-enough pregnancy.
And only one way you were birthed.
But there are daily hundreds of ways
to live & thousands of ways to die.
Sure, we had zero consciousness—
absolutely zero consciousness—
of the world prior to birth, but through
reading-fueled imagination, we can still
stroll through 1703 London in our tweed
waistcoats & smoke handrolleds, await
East India's latest calico shipment, & sip
the newest exotic tea in a window seat
as we listen to Newton's volatile, weekly
prognostications & revolutions at
the Royal Society down on Fleet Street.
We'll pound mugs & fists on the tabletops
when we disagree with him & sometimes
even when we agree. And after our
consciousness switches off for the final
time, we'll have no idea who the future
world-changers will be. We'll miss all
those next great ideas. And we won't
be the wiser for it. But that doesn't mean
we act with impunity or nihilism or
callousness. We can care a little less
without having to care about anything
& everything. It's called empathy
management. You should try it sometime,
without ever losing sight of who you are.
Who you're becoming. Enjoy becoming.
There are still some of us that still
care that you care as much as you do.
Will you take some advice from a stranger?
Will you take my hand? There's an escalator
around back. It doesn't need to be a tragic
fall, this tough transition. We can talk
along the way, maybe learn something
from each other. Maybe produce something
elegant. Or we can just move in silence,
our elbows occasionally, accidentally,
comfortably bumping each other, as we
stroll in this stay-in-the-moment silence.

Today Reminds Me

Of the TV's invisible wall in a side-scrolling
video game: the left-side barrier that presses
the mustachioed immigrant plumber only
forward, to the right, for there is no past,
no turning around—just a time-constrained
future: a relentless pursuit of eradicating
fungi, collecting loose change, inspecting
city sewers, & shrinking/enlarging as if
some fantastic Alice. But he could never
be Alice. Nor his brother. He'd never even
imagine wearing a green shirt—jealousy
of another, or even a previous incarnation
of himself, has never once entered his mind.
He can't ever go back, & today I'm 18 years
away from being 29 again. Today, I'm 18 years
away from 65. Today reminds me that almost
daily I drift back to some memory of my first
18 years, everything that Play-Doh shaped
or flattened: Lakewood to Fairview, Chautauqua
to Sanibel to the background Maxell mixed-tape
as I basement Nintendoed on the Berber with
George & Chris. But—recklessly—I've always
ceded too much power to self-consciousness
& too often propped up previous critics
from whom I'd never take advice today.
Like at class Confirmation, the only tan jacket
in a sea of navies. Or the first day of fourth grade.
Even now, I've a fear of that nun who threatened
at the end of her long bony index finger, *Mister,*
I'll jump down your throat & teeter on your wishbone.
What the hell does that even mean? And still part
of me wants to pummel Father Williams for telling
me *you'll never be smart enough* because who does
that to an anxious seventeen-year-old? Maybe less
anxiety at-that-point if I'd known I'd get to marry
at-some-point & have three kids at-other-points
with the magnetic girl who knows exactly how
to conquer worlds? Maybe less anxiety if the
in loco parentis teachers supposed to shepherd
me didn't take bites from the casserole
of me before I was even finished baking?
But I'm not food. I'm not hundreds of lizards
stacked up & wearing a human skin like

a certain Texas senator. No, I have ethics.
I'm no Russian nesting doll. Even if skin sloughs
& regenerates every 27 days, I remember now
—thanks to my therapist-mechanic-magician—
that within me I possess a remarkably resilient
machine whose steampunk gears click-spin-whirr
& realize that if time is indeed a wall, with calm
intent I can ghost float through it—zip back
to Grandma Mac hugging out my breath,
singing *cause I love you a bushel & a peck,*
& contentment can be finally realized
because there's liberation in imperfection:
perpetual duct tape, WD-40, Swiss Army Knife,
& fertilizer. And so, this past fall, instead of
raking replica ancient curbside burial mounds
like my neighbors, I left all the crumpled rough
drafts of wind-blown leaves in our flower beds.
I think I'll leave them there a while so the eggs
& larvae & potato bugs & caterpillars
have a further chance, & maybe in-turn
they'll make sure the wisteria blooms extra
fragrant come spring. As anxious as I am
to find out if it works, just knowing there's
real possibility in the soil…well…
that's more than enough for today.

II.

The Cosmos of Small Details: When A Young Poet Asked for Advice

For Dean Young (1955-2022)

Hey Bro, how do we know what's real?
Like what's really real? Can you actually
prove to me dinosaurs existed? Prove
evolution? Prove radio waves? Gravity,
rainbows, calculus, the water cycle,
Hi-Fi, Wi-Fi, or photosynthesis? Prove
camaraderie or credit or blame or
love or loathing or gods or ghosts or
trauma or pain or coping or the desperate
need to hold onto childhood agony
because that'll be the fuel for when you
invent the first internal combustion engine,
X-rays, the first wheel, bicycles, water
filters, germ theory, silk from worms
munching on mulberry leaves, global
trade routes, & altered migration patterns,
or plutonium or the device that'll allow
you to actually see molecules, atoms,
quarks, feelings, or how airplanes
or poets fly. Is there ever a day it
doesn't rain? Is there ever a day
without death? So everything must
become the proverbial grist for the mill.
Wait just a minute. Prove the tides,
the air stream, hurricanes versus
typhoons versus witches are only
witches if they drown—thin line
between fueling hysteria & being
brave enough to speak out against
the con being perpetuated. Such
thin lines among belief, emotion,
knowledge, power, & the abuse
of power, which basically describes
my Catholic upbringing. So, how

do we make sense of X? Where X
might be…reality, magic, & maybe
the idea of existence itself? 42 &
beyond 42. So how do we make
those authentic & magical connections
with others—whether it's in the form
of relationships or in writing itself?
Well… it may seem counterintuitive,
but the best way for beginning astronomers
to create a generalized-slash-shared
experience is by delving headlong
into the particulars of your very own
lived-slash-imagined experience: five
senses, props, proper nouns, soundtracks,
odd fascinations, weird peccadillos,
strange captivations, wild obsessions,
humble talents, & specific details
of precisely what happened. Through
particulars (not abstractions), you'll
connect with a small group of likeminded
freaks & like a stone tossed into a flat
pond, those connections will ripple out,
& maybe now those ripples are radio
waves out beyond the Milky Way, out
into the warm distances of the universe,
& you'll then connect even better with
an even broader audience. This is why
we tell beginning writers to show, not tell.
Showing allows us to experience… &…
just maybe… connect & experience
&-or empathize with you. Like walking
into a room suddenly filled with freshly
baked brownies. And your grandmother.
Who doesn't miss getting lost in the folds
of a hug from grandma? Or a pat on the back
from a lifechanging professor? It's not rocket
science; it's priceless rocket fuel. The fact is,
we'll all be dead soon. Living 75 years isn't
even a blip in our cosmic history. And so—
terribly—many of us aren't even guaranteed
that long. And there's about nothing more
ridiculous than using our precious seconds
to write our ridiculous poems. But their
ridiculousness is our culture is, in fact,
our time well-spent. Because we all

so desperately want to be remembered,
so why don't you give me something
to remember you-yes-you specifically by,
instead of being yet another person to
mimic-imitate-remember dead white
British hoity-toity poet X by. I already
remember them. And I'd like to remember
you, too, you bleeping weirdo. Because this
is what we're really trying to get at, right?
To connect to people who think like us—
making the ordinary extraordinary or
magic-wanding the extraordinary into
the ordinary—even if it's a galactically
small pool of people who think like us.

Dear Sadness,

For Vedran Smailović, Tomaso Albinoni, & Remo Giazotto

You didn't begin with a tuxedoed musician in the grey brick dust of the bombed-out bakery storefront ruins in Sarajevo; the cello wasn't invented only for you, but gosh she sure has you fully figured out as she moans the *Adagio in G Minor*. Longing is the door to belonging, which is why, despite the rubble of my faith, I still love church music, incense, & stained glass, especially the mournful chorus of Christmas melodies. Silent night. Holy night. Through insomniac nights I've come to see much of my anxiety is either fear or excitement, excitement that I get to engage someone-thing new—we will talk about those things that, frankly, make me excited, like the quiet dissection of you—fear that I'm going to be let down again, that I'm going to see the world for how it really is: rubble, arrangements to make more rubble, planning stages for rising from the rubble. Seeing just how disappointing people can be. You unite us, Sadness. You are the vagal nerve & Darwin as promoter of survival of the compassionate, for after all what's-a-picnic-what's-communion without pathos? I want to long because I'm at my best when I'm longing. Will we ever learn to appreciate those that believe there isn't more than this? That excuse construction of terror & sadness through construction of an afterlife instead of appreciating the small beauty of a light shaft cutting through the debris cloud? Of course, not all tragedies are my tragedy to explain, to make sense of on others' behalf, but also, ignoring tragedy perpetuates future tragedy. We can always find an excuse when we're looking for excuses. Loss' lessons as journeys instead of destinations; longing morphs into belonging when we slow time, allow it to elongate, allow ourselves to find fellowship in you.

Arithmetic Word Problem: On Turning Fifty

We're creeping up on 120 billion
people who have ever lived, with
about 15% of those, alive now. We
think that's a lot, but if each of us
is a grain of sand, that's only enough
sand to fill a swimming pool that's
44 feet long & 22 feet wide & 4.5
feet deep. Yeah, I did the math.
I did the math because we're always
thinking that if we can measure it,
we can give it meaning. Mass &
volume & time. Carbon & helium &
hydrogen & nitrogen & silica & oxygen.
And yet, we'd never call ourselves sand.
Instead, we tend to think we're the shell
stuck in that sand, the shell that's half-
in-half-out, emerging not retreating,
pearlescent & brilliantly painted by
nature & standing like a monument—
like a tree, as much visible as invisible,
waiting for a sunrise beachcomber
as the waves ebb on that island that
we can't get back to soon enough.
That beach we think about as we
caress the hollows & points of our
trophy shells that now sit in the
crystal bowl in the living room.
Collecting dust. Those shells aren't
toys but are daydreams & memories.
Sorry to tell you, but we're not that
heirloom shell, either. We're never
the lettered olive, lightning whelk,
or banded tulip we think we are.
We're not even the cascading mix
of sand & surf who offered up that
gorgeous husk. We're only the sand's
dust, motes spinning through this
weird universe on our round rock
that for all purposes shouldn't
even exist. Fluke explosion. Rock
among other rocks. Orb circling
other orbs at incomprehensible
miles per hour. Poof. Proof of

something-anything is all we
ask for.... Alright fine. All right,
how about this? How about the fact
that our rock is the only one with
wine. And art. And poetry. And
running & lush gardens & warm
rain & black basalt cobblestone streets
& tiramisu & hugs & a wife's electric
laughter & daughters laugh-crying
into each other's shoulders. And
love. God, there's just so much
& so little at the same time. And so,
I think about all the people who
didn't get to fifty, the tinkling tide
pulling them back to the depths
far too soon. I think of all those
grains of sand & beaches I've
dipped my toes into & shells I've
passed by or picked up or connected
with or caught a lustrous glint of
as another breathtaking sunrise
greeted me. Gosh, any day we see
the sunrise is a good day. And I'm
grateful. I'm just so terribly grateful.

A History of the People Who've Shaped Me, Even When They Weren't Trying to Shape Me

He looks like the sort of fella who's wearing
overalls even when he's not wearing overalls.
And he looks like an astronomer gazing into
the distance, even if he's just trying to remember
my name. She looks like she's just caught up on
the laundry even though a family's laundry
is never complete because life is a constant battle
with dirt, unless you live outside, & in that case,
you're not really dirty unless your fingers are
actively hoeing the flower bed. Don't let her
delicate flower demeanor fool you. And her?
She's always about to gossip even when there's
little truth to anything she repeats. And he looks
constipated, even when he's not, & she looks
like she smells like lilac in her purple V-neck,
but I'd recommend an ample social distance.
Her, over there, on the other hand, she looks
like she's about to orgasm even if a good-oh-god
orgasm is not in her near future. Honey, never
be ashamed of buying the battery value pack.
And him? He looks like a city slicker, even
though his slickness undermines his slickness.
And he looks like he's thinking even when—
& she's about to fall asleep even though sleep
entirely eludes her after 3am. And he's going
to ask to borrow a tool, even if he is one. He looks
like he's going to ask for a favor, even if he isn't,
& sure he'll pay you back Tuesday for what you
surrender today, but just as there's an endless cycle
of Tuesdays, so too, if you're not careful, is endless
surrender. Kindness is more often manipulated
than rewarded. Her lips are moving as if she's
praying, even though she's not believed since
the eighth grade. He's scheming. She's plotting.
They are adding up what you owe, even if
you've been careful to owe no one anything.
No is enough. No doesn't need explanation.
You owe them no rationale. And he looked
confident in what he knew, but his loudness
was ample evidence that he was nothing more
than a large, hollow vessel capable of a lot of
noise. A small pebble echoing down an open,

empty manhole. The milk crate looked like
furniture, even when it wasn't trying to be.
The tree was just trying to be a tree. I'm still
wonderstruck that early explorers looked at
the untamed forests of the new world, trees
of Nova Scotia, Maine, the Carolinas, &
the Alaskan archipelago, & did not see—
did not see—the people, the animals, oxygen
& mossy plant balance, but looked upon
the natural flying buttresses & imagined
those needled & leafed columns for a future
world-colonizing navy. And so he looked like
he was constantly sucking lemons, even during
the South's deep freeze. His chin-first demeanor
disguising the fact of his glass jaw. And him?
Well, he's always tilted on his tiptoes, seeking
the future, even if his gripes anchor him
to the past. She's a princess. He's just been
hurt. They've just been diagnosed even when
the diagnosis is constantly changing. Science
most looks like science when it's uncertain.
To the Nth degree for maturity & being learned.
Which holds true for grammar, too. We cling
to it because of its promise of certainty,
but heck even that evolves for the better,
eventually—just ask he/him she/her they/them
zie/zim. And so, her appreciative eyes looked like
she was slicing onions, even when there were
no onions near. I said no onions near. No onions
nor allergens near, & why can't you realize
your desire not to look vulnerable makes you look
more vulnerable? Resting bitch face doesn't make
me think you're at all rested or aggressive,
so much as hurt & not getting the therapy
you need. Why can't you just articulate that
you want to be left alone? Your desire to hoard
power, your desire to turn everything into
a crusade makes no one want to crusade
with you, no one want to confide in you,
everyone want to strip you of those small things
you take pride in that not even your own mother
is proud of. And he looks as if he's eating hot wings
but he's really just speaking in public. And he,
well he's staring at a fishing bobber, waiting…
waiting… waiting… waiting… even though

he's in the middle of a metropolis. She's guns
& concrete & steel even though she's really
daisies & soil & horses. The idea you thought
was a grape gumdrop was really black licorice.
The milk on your Captain Crunch spoiled.
The neighbor not neighborly even slightly.
What happened to returning a wave? I let you
merge in front of me in traffic, I expect a
peace sign instead of a bird instead of apathy.
That wine label & price tag is little indication
of the headache you'll have in the morning.
And there's a coffin-maker masquerading
as a carpenter. An ambulance as a hearse.
When every squirrel looks like a potential pet,
cuddly or not. When every virus has the power
to kill you, even if it doesn't. Someone ready
to explain to, speak for, or think about,
even when decidedly unwanted. He looks like
he's always going to mansplain, even if he's
the furthest thing from manhood. And that
looks handcrafted, even if it's one in a thousand
from today's glowing forge. Bubbles. Fine art.
Economy. Humility undercutting humility.
And dust to dust. That looks like a theory
without an ounce of practice. And his forehead
is an architectural ornament, akin to the gleam
from the Chrysler Building, even if he's never
set foot in Manhattan. From a cave to a wigwam
to an opulent railroad car to a space shuttle.
Art Deco disguised as timeless. Concern for
others sold as socialism. One shelter needn't
look like another shelter. Her speech carries
the cut of an axe even when she's trying to soothe.
Intervention. Invention. Insurrection. And he looks
like he's suffering an indignity when he doesn't
know the meaning of suffering. He smells like
a civilized man, especially when he's trying to
masque savagery. The type that would sleep
with everyone even if he's yet to love anyone.
Including himself. Sweating. Lusting. Undressing
with eyes even though he just has an astigmatism.
Guilty when not. And her lips are always parted,
as if she's about to sing, even if she's tone deaf.
And he always has an idea, even if he can never
find the words to articulate said idea. What first

looked like a metaphor trying a little too hard
not to be a metaphor suddenly dropped its guise,
& left standing there was truth. At least one
incarnation of it. And so, when I'm gone, don't
let them put makeup on me so others say, "Oh,
he looks so natural," when—clearly—natural
is dead. But do know happiness as the goal
rarely works, nor does comparison for the sake
of comparison. And one of my biggest moments
of enlightenment came when I wasn't seeking it.
It's when I realized I'm not competing with you—
not competing with you, not competing with you.
A relief even when I wasn't looking for relief.

Willy Loman Syndrome

Will you continue to lie to your sons,
your wife, your dead brother's ghost,
your garden seeds, off-brand Frigidaire,
flute, or on-brand Studebaker; your
insurance agent, patched ceiling
& bungalow among skyscrapers
& neighborhood card game &
temporariness of a loan or what
wealth actually is, or to a gasline,
how much what fuels us can kill us,
or to your confidant or neighbor's kid
or idea of successful parenting &/or
how little adolescent sporting success
actually matters or to happiness itself
or to a secretary or boss or buyer
who lusts after silk stockings more
than your quickly fading but more
likely never there bedroom prowess
& to fidelity itself & to funeral dirt
& who may come & who likely won't
& the difference between mercurial
& just being honest with yourself
or anyone, for once, even if trapped
in an era where depression isn't
just a stigma but also isn't yet
understood for what it truly is
& just what are you trying to sell—
mythmaking itself & sometimes,
if you chase a dream, can you really
be all that surprised that if/when
you finally catch it, it turns out
to be just a dream?

My Superpower is Waking Up at 3am & Not Falling Back Asleep No Matter What I Do

The one certainty in tiger tracks:
follow them long enough & you will
eventually arrive at a tiger,
unless the tiger arrives at you first.
Russian Proverb
Quoted from John Vaillant's *The Tiger* (2010)

Did you know Amur Tigers can hear
the difference between an airplane engine
& the *thwat-thwat-thwat* of a landing helicopter
& have been known to leap from trees
to swat at the hunters before the chopper
struts even hit the forest floor? Did you
know this same tiger might even know
your scent, left behind on part of her boar kill,
when you only meant to take a hind shank,
just enough to stave off your stomach grumble,
but that was her hind shank, & now she's
capable of tracking your Old Spice 10 kilometers,
first destroying the outhouse where she can
still smell her boar, even in your excrement,
& paw into your lean-to, transforming
the stuffing inside your mattress into
dandelion puff blown across the Russian
river valley, & she keeps stalking you,
not being as evasive as you need to be?
You can't shake who you are, laying there
thinking that thinking about too much
of the past fuels depression, & thinking
too much of the future, anxiety. Depression
& anxiety: one's hunting you; the other
already has you mounted on her wall
in the study. What if the *thwat-thwat-thwat*
decides it's your turn next? Do we all gotta
take our turn in the barrel? This has nothing
to do with William Blake's innocence. It has
to do with perspective, with realizing that if
a tiger could talk, like most travelers from
an antique land, we wouldn't understand
her language. Heck, we barely understand
each other's. And man's artificial kingdoms—
all of them—will eventually fall, time the great

nullifier of supposedly impermeable borders,
& yet Sharpie-carrying politicians still disguise
themselves as authoritative cartographers.
And so, in 1909 Estonian Jakob von Ueküll
used biology to explain human behavior &
society's structure, likely thought-up at 3am:
Umwelt coexists with *Umgebung. Umgebung* is
the objective environment around us: the shops
& cart vendors & fire hydrants & potholes
& lampposts along the sidewalks we all
share. But but but, this objective environment
is really only theoretical, right? Because while
place might seem objective & well-mapped
& glass & steel & concrete, because we
all have different *umwelt*, our experiences
of the "real" world, the *umgebung*, are actually
all very different. You still with me? You dig?
So if the *umgebung* is the concrete world,
the *umwelt* is the different colored soap bubbles
surrounding each of us, each biological creature,
each sealed in our own tinted bubble floating
through the world. So, her umwelt is rose-colored
like her spectacles, & his is gray because
he's never happy unless he's unhappy,
& another's surrounding soap bubble
is yellow because he's either cowardly or
too cheery—never a middle ground. Anyway,
like a model of spray-painted Styrofoam atoms
forming molecules for a grade school science fair
project, we all bumble down the sidewalk
in our own luminous or dingy umwelts.
Umwelts through the umgebung. A mother
& puppy through the suburb, "While she might
be keenly aware of a sale sign in the window,
a policeman coming toward her, or a broken
bottle in her path," the puppy she's walking,
in his own, faintly fuchsia bubble, "would focus
on the gust of cooked meat emanating from
a restaurant's exhaust fan, the urine on
the fire hydrant, & doughnut crumbs
next to the broken bottle." These two
are in the same umgebung, but their different
umwelt give them vastly different experiences
of it. These two parallel universes share
commonalities: both puppy & woman

need to be careful crossing the road, both
notice another approaching dog, both perceive
the cop, but given their different umwelten,
they notice, perceive, attend to the environment
for different reasons, even if those soap bubbles
sometimes overlap. He's hungry. She's not.
Stomachs growl or don't. Thin blue line means
nothing to a dachshund. You know what's
also cool? We can step into each other's
bubbles—human or animal—& our familiar
is *abracadabra presto-change-o* transformed:
we can see the world as another sees it.
Biology—from potato bugs to crows to wild
boars to hunters & prey—inspires…
if we uncork our minds, make our umwelt
bubbles permeable at 3am, or in our afternoon
strolls through town, urban forest, a reverse
rainstorm of multicolored helium balloons,
ascending & bumping & merging &
maybe, just maybe, we find understanding…
because we'll no longer be prisoners of our
subjective bubbles. Successful hunting is
an act of terminal empathy. Successful
empathy, an act of relentless imagination.

Empathy Hotel

My dad couldn't ever beat up your dad.
It's not that he's not tough; it's just that
he's older & grayer now, big-headed &
bookish. Mild mannered & nonviolent.
And other than at poorly refereed ballgames
or the oblivious waiter ghosting his table
or the airline once again misplacing his
suitcase, seat, airplane, patience, or kindness,
he's rarely yelled at anyone about anything.
Besides, who hasn't felt better after a good
Munchian-scream into the existential oblivion
& then subsequent-immediate-overtipping-
overapologizing guilt about humiliating
that kid just trying to scrape by who actually
has little control over *waves arm* any
of this? And even if it's not a competition,
he has likely stayed in more hotels than your
dad ever could. Airline miles as the measure
of a man. A documentary doesn't promise
truth as we're always choosing the POV
from which to tell the story. Which facts
to include or omit. As when daily our brains
ignore the image of our noses, so we're not
constantly looking to see the points of
our noses. Please don't look at your nose.

You looked at your nose, didn't you?
Pareidolia is when you think you see
a face in your grapefruit, toast, tree,
potatoes, or clouds. It happens all
the time. As when you think you see
Jesus Christ in the bathroom floor tiles
or Richard Nixon in the walnut stump
just outside the window—if you lean
& squint just right. It might even be
the face of your own father reappearing
when you least expect it. But that
vestigial imagination was really useful
once upon a time, as when the maternal
caveman version of you thought she saw
a lion lurking in the grass, but it just turned
out to be the sway of the grain against
the autumnal setting sun & you freaked

out for nothing. That freak out cost you
goosebumps, a sprint, & elevated heartrate,
but if your brain had ignored the lion image
& it wasn't in fact an image but a lion,
you might not be here now, & thus we
all might not be here now. That's basically
how Ancestry DNA works, our survival
hitchhiking on the radio waves of what
we think we see or hear. [This is me
omitting a fact.] There used to be
a local radio spot aired around the holidays
which encouraged absentee fathers to go
home for the holidays—*because sometimes
presence is enough*—but there wasn't one
of those super-fast-talking lawyers at
the commercial's end cataloging all the
caveats. Asterisks for all the facts that
include the fact that sometimes presence
includes intoxications, humiliations, or
toxic masculinity. But inside our home those
things weren't my dad—were they yours?
Is it okay if I'm sorry if they were yours?
Daily I do all I can not to look down my nose.
In fact, Dad cried, hugged, kissed & *I love you'd*
more than Mom. Essentially, they were
a cost-benefit construct of privilege versus
presence. Strength through vulnerability.
Maybe absence of evidence is what's
preferable? During our 40 years of growing
up Dad traveled 5-6 nights per week.
Mom held us together as most cave
societies were wont to do. I don't hold
resentment like another sibling, as we
wanted for little, his guilt a great motivator
for stuff, stuff no replacement for time
spent, but his time sacrifice was a biological
documentary about how one generation
sacrifices for the next, but also as a result,
now I'm definitely not an intermittent father.
Vulnerability embedded in our unbreakable
evolutionary chain. When the absence of
evidence is used as evidence of what's about
to happen, as when a supremacist Army officer
used absence as proof, justification for all those
internment camps, converted horse stalls
at Santa Anita not even thinly disguised

as hotel rooms: *evidence proves that they*
haven't conspired just yet. But that lack
of conspiring proves they are conspiring. I.e.,
the fact that sabotage hasn't been undertaken
is proof that sabotage will be undertaken.
Or some such horrific & bigoted nonsense.
Even New Deal & war-winning FDR
had his catastrophes, as if any of us
can really be heroes. We're too quick
to choose our heroes, too slow to disavow
the ones who've morally erred, & often use
a quest for perfection as an excuse for our
undealt with anxieties & illnesses & therapist
avoidance. Hollow & incurious men,
you double-downers on being wrong—
the opposite of my own father in almost
every way—don't you realize your lack
of curiosity isn't commendation-worthy?
It's always better to be a learner than it is
to be learned. This is me trying to explain,
not sabotage, my own parenting style,
omitting little, perhaps risking too much.
And so, his issue with customer service
becomes your issue with customer service,
& since we can't always complain to
a president or a savior or a father… well
I suppose we can, but is he even listening?
Listen, not that everything is a competition,
but I can overthink you under the table.
We are basically a family of Olympian
overthinkers. And feelers. And now,
evolution-in-an-instant later, we're
terrible at predicting text & we're
even worse with all those new faces
& names. Truly, only once in my life
have I meant to type *mother ducking*.
And next time you bump into him,
please tell old-what's-his-face from
the old neighborhood that I said, *Hello*
&
Please tell him when he stopped trying
to be precise & perfect & instead decided
to just be flawed & vulnerable, to own it
& adapt & commit to learning better,
I finally started to see just how complete
love could be.

Prolific Ghost Fuel

For Dean Young (1955-2022): Cor Cordium.
And for Dobby, Jamie, Karen, Chrissy, Allison, & William.

The five-point palm exploding heart
technique, quite simply, is the deadliest
blow in all of martial arts. He hits you
with his fingertips at five different
pressure points on your body, & then
lets you walk away. But once you've
taken five steps, your heart explodes
inside your body & you fall to the floor,
dead. One space, no longer two, end
punctuation. The same thing happens
when someone who inspires you dies,
even if it's been a minute or decade
since you told him so. The *CliffsNotes*
version of *The Remains of the Day* equal,
Wait! I may have misperceived the
people & values I built my entire life
around. Upon. Inside a friendship
I discovered a teacher with relentless
belief in his flock. Transpose the last
sentiment. The falsity of the exclamation
point because only after we see it
do we realize that we were supposed
to be excited from the start. No do
overs & you're out of mulligans.
And what the day remains are, are
the hours left after you do everything
busy busy busy & then in the evening
you finally get to sit in your favorite
chair with that favorite drink & the cat
that's shitty to everyone but you & you're
finally present in that stress-releasing
moment rather than busy busy busy.
Maybe stop using *busy* as an excuse
to take a break from caring so much?
We all want to be a comma, not a full
stop, but in all likelihood we're just
another unanswered question mark,
negatively capable more than positive,
more unpositive-red-squiggly-line,
unsure of anything ever anywhere.

How Microsoft Word now dictates
mechanics, copyedits, & since Word
is now the lead vehicle in the parade
of interpersonal communication &
since communication is the vehicle
connecting the battery terminals to
your friendship, the truth is now
algorithm updates are seeping into
if & how we tell those we love that
we love them—in a way they'll always
remember. Soon enough we're all
CliffsNotes, obituaries of longing.
Spoiler: it takes two movies to finally
kill him. A collection of all the moments
right before the moment where everything
changes. Dear Teacher, whose name
isn't written in water? Woven through
it? So, we tell him. So we tell them.
We tell them in a way that when
we finally do walk away, just before
we take that fifth step, we remember,
they remember our earnest & electric
gratitude for the fact that the last thing
they did for us was to lay their hand,
gently & violently, across our chest.

III.

If the Water Molecules Making Up X Change Moment-by-Moment, Then the Banks & Locale Surely Define a River, Right?

In some cultures
if the deceased
is cremated,
it's taboo to spread
ashes in the creek
stream pond lake sea,
as the deceased's
soul will forever
be unsettled, as
water rarely stops
traveling. But as I
lack a soul—a fact
first floated by
the nuns at St. Mark's
Elementary—I'm
content with unsettled,
& honestly, a bit
enchanted that
eventually—once I'm
unceremoniously
dumped into the
Cuyahoga—my
molecules will flow
past the fords
floodgates locks bilges
& faucet filters,
& into all of you.
Raises glass
So...
cheers.

How Little I Know Of How Things Really Work In Florence

Sure, I like Medusa's hairdo well enough, even if Michelangelo's *David* isn't also at Uffizi. And I know where to buy jewelry, even if it's not in the budget & never will be, but I can still drink authentic espresso like an ersatz Italian, as if most truths aren't fleeting. Machiavelli, Mike, & Galileo are buried in Santa Croce, half a block from our musty 5th floor walkup Airbnb. But I don't know the Florentine garbage schedule, the non-touristy sandwich shops, the cops to know or avoid, or the real biases hiding under the stereotypes. As when the Irish really only hate two things in this world: people who are intolerant of other people's cultures. And the English. Can I really still be arrested for blasphemy? I don't know the Tuscan protocol for saying, These shrines aren't working. For saying, My kid is sick & needs help & I'm not sure how to provide it, despite the therapists & psychiatrists & medications & escapism, both international & imagined, & deep breathing, so much of the painfully deep breaths, for all, if not one. Sure, I like the Duomo well enough, & I appreciate the centuries-long tussle with the French about who actually invented the fleur-de-lis, but can you please point me in the right direction? I can't remember the name of the piazza—where do I find the monument to mental health?

Wanna Know How Geography's Helped with Anxiety?

For Coco

Two main things. First,
there are two US states
bordered by no other
state. And one state
that's bordered by only
one state: Maine is boxed
in by New Hampshire,
so if by train, Chucks,
boots, skis, or wheels,
you ain't going in unless
New Hampshire first lets
you in. Or if you chopper,
swim, sail, or Canada. And
just look at how beautiful
Maine is, with her single
protector. Next, India has
1.4 billion people. That's
almost 4x the people in
our country & 82x
the people in our little
suburban community,
& at most, a person
can only manage 150
relationships at once,
& here & now none
are the blessed people
in India. And likely,
by the time I kick, if
I'm fortunate I'll meet
a couple dozen of India's
people on her turf, but
more likely, they'll never
know I exist. And that's
kinda liberating.

Nine Weeks In

For Annie

Forty-two UPS trucks pass us on the highway,
& urgency has never presented itself to me
like this before: the browns & golds mosaic
into an opaque curtain, & you are all thought,
all aura & atmosphere, an idea inside my wife
inside a car, entering or leaving a corporation limit,
ducking the landing planes, squirting through
another county, at swimming peace, taking in
David Bowie on the radio, eyeless, yet capable
of bringing me to tears with the thought of filling
your head with bad space movies, plutonium,
translucence, a Buzz Aldrin anecdote to instruct
you against jealousy. You'll be able to escape
from Germany at the end of WWII to build
rockets for America, play Rachmoninov for
the ice skaters in the park because the music
always changes, & like music you can alter
moods by simply existing. You have power,
but don't know how to wield it. You are not
the water melting, but the actual slip on the ice,
that intangible in-between that occurs instantly
& can't be held. And all I want to do is hold you.
You are not my flat globe of limitation. You are not
vain about your hair yet, only downy & sprouting.
Tooth buds & touchpads. You are Lord Byron
in space because you are adventure, scope,
& enough caricature to accomplish such a feat.
You need no reasons. You will see rain as energetic,
judgement as vital, & elevators in everyone.
You don't know time, only bloat & burble. Tinge
& pricked skin. We're just learning what life is.

Travel Tip #3: Antarctica & Growth

If you stand at the South Pole
& take a step in any direction,
you'll be headed north. If you
stand at the South Pole & take
a step in any direction, you'll
be headed north, & if you keep
going, you'll end up in very
different places. If you stand
at the South Pole & take
a step in any direction,
you'll be headed north,
& if you keep going, you'll
end up in very different places,
& you'll never get to take
that first step a second time,
& you'll learn to be okay
with that because canoes
or ocean freighters. Hot air
balloons or Zeppelins or
biplanes or Concords or
space capsules, & next thing
every place you've ever been
will take a new shape, each
jungle leaf not just a leaf,
but maybe a canopy, each
spice not just a spice, but
maybe a currency, each
raindrop a potential drink,
snowflake, or tear; each
cityscape not just a skyline,
but maybe a memory.
Not just a memory, but
an invisible & teeming
with life magnetic field,
equal parts repulsion
& attraction.

Home Improvement

I discovered a single long wave
of your black Irish hair
stuck to the first coat
of gloss white oil
on the living room's baseboard.
Rather than remove it
with the tweezers
of my bent index & scarred thumb,
I tucked the filament's end
onto the quarter round,
& with a steady angled cut-in,
on a second pass,
fossilized your DNA
into our planet.
When the alien scientists
come back in 3,000 years,
rather than search for persistence
in amber, a la *Jurassic Park,*
they can extract it
from just above the floor,
the maple hardwoods still shining.
A whole theme park of Bridgets
will be difficult to contain.
And while I'll be long gone,
it'll be one of those attractions
no one will ever look away from,
& why would they want to?

Even With Proof, Victorians Were Less Willing to Believe in Michael Faraday's Never-Heard-of-Before *Electromagnetic Field* Than They Were an Early Version of Ouija Boards

A parlor room fad called *table-turning*
gripped London in the 1850s, & to turn
a table a séance-like group would sit
around said table & attempt to summon
& form authentic-yet-mystical connections
with the other side's spirits, as often this
side's non-answers aren't at all satisfying,
& so everyone place your hands your palms
down flat, light the candles, plume the incense,
& chant aloud the alphabet & maybe the table
will tilt, rotate, or wobble toward answers,
this conjuring, this hands-on evidence
of mesmerism, our sacred inanimate objects
twitching via ghostly powers. Bunk
debunk bunk. Then in July 1853 Faraday
slyly put some séance tables on rollers,
observed their immovability, tricking
the tricksters, the cold truth revealed
during the next night's spectacle
turned spectacleless, & soon after
published a cited article exposing
the charlatans. It took many of
the superstition's believers almost
a decade to believe him. And even
today, superstition outsells electricity
& magnets. When aren't we trying
to make the unseen seen? When aren't
we hoping others will behave thoughtfully
toward us, even if/when we're not fully
present anymore? Even if every ghost
is just a memory or a desperate desire,
is being remembered really too much
to ask for?

When International Travel Makes You Feel Like You're a Time Traveler

In part because you're sipping espresso
or wine inside a deconsecrated church
with original frescos 6 hours ahead
of where you usually rest your head
& you pop onto a news website & see
there's been another shooting targeting
the already-marginalized but you've not
been even a little marginalized because
of how you look, even if you don't *ciao ciao*
like the rest of the patrons & because
of your too pink complexion & short
black trench coat you keep getting
confused for an Englishman & yes
the leather store proprietor confirms
that that's better than being American
because they are so stuck in the Wild
West past thinking they're battling to take
the land-culture from the indigenous *kapow*
kapow & isn't it nice to roam the streets &
not feel like your rights or lives are about
to be—*didn't you all already fight that*
battle? Why do you keep looking for more?

IV.

Travel Tip #42: For When You Stumble Upon a Time Machine

You take another step toward the phonebooth
& with its abundance of cast-iron-framed-little
windows, the kiosk almost looks torn from
a between-the-wars London avenue, but its
burnished silver-gold Chrysler Building
Art Deco embellishments unsubtly hint
at something special. You step inside.
The weight of the air feels momentous,
full of more gravity, as when you step
inside St. Peter's Basilica, the Louvre,
or through the giant wooden train doors
at Mauthausen. Amazing how architecture
& archeology can create awe-filled tears.
You survey the three sets of beveled gages:
DD/MM/YYYY, time, location. Awaiting
input, flashing neon chases itself, & the one-
armed slot machine lever awaits your
handshake. Just how far back into history
could you travel, to any place on the planet,
& still have your carefully-chosen-pseudo-
Neil-Armstrong-greeting-in-English
be understood by the awaiting scout,
delegation, masses, or apes, when you
vacuum-whoosh exit? Maybe they're
curious. Maybe angry. Maybe pantaloons,
thobes, togas, or deer pelts, & maybe they
are prepping your deification ceremony:
lutes & pipes & timbrels & wine & garland
& livestock sacrifice & communal cooking pot
& wild ecstasy & unheard melodies. Because
who doesn't wonder… always, always partly
through a lens of narcissism, even if fleeting?
You're either eating from the pot, or you're
in it. So how far back, anywhere in the world,
& which two words from current culture

could you utter to that civilization & still
be understood? Well, the answers are these:
A.) you can go back into history about 6,000
years; B.) you can land virtually anywhere
on the globe that's inhabited & very likely
you'll always be understood, be empathized
with, or prove a human truth about relatability
just by saying, C.) [illegible] or [illegible]

Some Cultures Use the Same Word for *Blue & Green*

When I heard the commotion
on the front porch, I swung open
the frontal lobe-I-mean-door,
expecting an Amazon package—
printer ink for a document
professionally vital & until
that exact moment, perilously
procrastinated; yet, at my feet,
I instead found a retractable
ramp extended from my next
step to the bubble hubcap
looking spaceship parked
on my just-fertilized lawn,
& on that shiny silver corridor,
about midway between the ship
& my stoop was a Great Gazoo
looking dude, about 5'11" &
dusty blonde, almost a perfect
reflection of me, if not for his
algae green complexion. And
in perfect Midwestern, Hello
Dum-dum, where would you
like to go first, huh? What
would you like to see? Among
the fused helium & hydrogen,
nitrogen & nebula, corkscrew
galaxies & distant & smoky
big bang epicenter, what proof
do you need first? What exotic
food? What alien art? What
hierarchy of good, banality
of evil, or shared pastries
& smiles in a distant café
despite the foreign tongues
do you first need in order
to affirm that everything
you'll ever need was, is,
& will always be, right on
this very doorstep?

Meet & Greet with Zaphod Beeblebrox

Part of my brain wasn't super surprised
by this morning's TMZ announcement,
NASA & ESA & CNSA confirmed: there's
an Earth-similar planet with proof-of-life
seven galaxies over —they are interstellar
radio savvy, in the very least. And yeah,
they've been in contact for about two years,
& after this latest pandemic the powers
that be finally think we're ready for the big
news because as a species we obviously
can't panic more than we already have,
& besides, do you really think we are
really capable of unmucking-things-up
all on our own? That our diplomatic ship
will include 100 non-astronaut humans
is a bit more surprising. Supposedly,
we're meeting up 42 years after blastoff
at a mid-universe Starbucks. So, despite
my mild propensity toward motion
sickness, I sat down to update my résumé
& to email for recommendation letters,
but now I'm thinking about getting on
the hiring committee instead, as the
impact hazard & cost-benefit analysis
were already decided, & the possibility
of exploiting Mars' diamond-stuffed soil
& platinum-laced asteroids were deemed
a lower priority than curiosity, for once.
But which 100 will be worthy? The ultimate
Olympics: 8+ billion across 200 nations
enter the arena, fewer than half
the flags will take the podium, most likely
the powerbrokers with a small entourage.
But what earns powerbroker status?
Nuclear weapons? Mutually assured
destruction an acceptable trade-off for
the ship's fuel because solar energy
obviously ain't going to cut it in the void
of deep dark cold spaces inside space?
And what should they take with them?
Music, from Chuck Berry to whale songs,
religious pamphlets, photos & videos,
Grandpa's gold-trimmed-leather-bound

encyclopedia collection covered in dust
in my attic because none of us had
the heart to put it on the curb with the
wagon wheels & treadworn Goodyears?
What's the recipe for a galactic time
capsule? As in, *Here are all the things that*
make Earthlings, Earthlings. Is every
person really a different person? And,
like any revelation of truth, how many
collective warts do we expose, keeping
in mind they may have been listening,
scrolling our internet, & they may
be behind our plethora of cats, cat
videos, & the deification of cats
by cats. As well as the Siri/Alexa
algorithm that suggests what to buy
based on overheard conversations.
Likely, now, more cat toys. No need
to thank me. They also may be further
along in their history, & their societal
stratification might be right-side-up.
On their planet, which skin pigments
are atop the social ladder? Is their
nuanced geo-political history mostly
an encyclopedia of powerful women,
however they socially construct gender?
What do they exchange for currency?
Are they still on shells & wampum?
Did they realize the basics are more
than enough? Coinage & paper &
e-currency just showing off, placing
more value in excess never necessary.
I mean sure, culture is all the things
we don't need but still have/do/buy,
including elaborately garnished curry
dishes & art, which is the most enduring
symbol of humanity, enough for thousands
of museums & a once upon a time library
in Alexandria. Which paintings should we
send? Do we send what's derivative
because you know, learning is about
being derivative & to ignore
derivation in favor of divination
is the peak delusion of self-importance.
What kind of lifespan are they talking

about? Have they advanced to, *I'll take your word for it, Spaceman?* Are their moons more revered because they are capable of self-shining in darkness? Their suns diminished because how special are suns when they only shine in daylight anyway? Before leaving this pale blue dot, I'd ask you just three simple questions: 1.) What have you created? 2.) Can you tell me about a significant relationship in your life? 3.) What suffering have you overcome & how did you do it? Even if we are like butterflies who flutter for a day & think it is forever, take all the time you need to explain your answers. Help yourself to the communal water cooler in the corner, should you get thirsty or need more time to think, & in the meantime, the cats won't keep you company.

“The Ships Hung in the Sky Much in the Same Way that Bricks Don’t”

Quoted from Douglas Adams’ *Hitchhiker’s Guide to the Galaxy* (1979)

The chips crunched in the mouth
much in the same way that yogurt
doesn’t, & yet her homemade
pudding crunched on my molars
much in the same way gravel might.
She tried to poison her spouse much
in the same way soulmates don’t,
& they first made love much in
the same way people with extra
limbs & little coordination might,
marionettes marionetted by other
marionettes, an infinite line of strings
& janky elbows elbowing their way
into somehow always being in the way
& thus their offspring acknowledged
their lineage much in the same way
royalty would never not acknowledge.
The car stopped in the road much
in the same way boats don’t, & so
they avoided accumulating snow
much in the same way the city’s
plow trucks do. His meaning in life
was clear much in the same way
a stained-glass window filters light
at 6 o’clock on a Northeast Ohio
January evening. The brain functioned
much in the way seamless garments
don’t. The eyebrows furrowed much
in the same way cliches are unique.
And so a new commandment was
born: the only acceptable furrow to
date is, “He furrowed his brow until
you could grow some of the smaller
root vegetables in it.” Yes, of course it’s
proper that in today’s culture to compare
any person to any vegetable ought
to be cause for cancellation, but on
the subject of vegetables, don’t ask
me to consume them again until
their resume is as diversified
as the potato’s. Get out of here

with your cauliflower pretending
to be bread & pasta much in the same
way aluminum foil decides it's delicious.
Furthermore, the Cleveland Browns
footballed much in the same way
champions don't. Ditto for the baseball
club. And basketball team, save one
miracle, & the city, for that matter,
developed the lakefront much in the
same way Chicago, or any prosperous
& gleaming waterfront town, didn't.
I balanced our checkbook much in the
manner teeter totters don't because
finances make sense to me much in
the same way as astrophysics' subgenre
helioseismology does. The pillow soothed
his face much in the way her hair doesn't,
the stray strand tickling his cheek just
under his eye, & so he slept much
in the same way overcaffeinated
overthinkers do. And couples in movies
make out in the morning before brushing
their teeth much in the same way no real
couple with a proper sense of smell, taste,
& gag reflex ever could. And so when
she propped herself up on her elbow
& asked him, "What do you think?"
He responded by saying, "I think
a 100-pound dog is a pretty big dog."
And from that point forward whenever
he asked her, "What are you doing
with that?" She responded with, "I'm
training it to like whatever I'm doing
with it." In that way they began to
communicate with each other not with
love, or words of love, or all the little
details & actions of love, but love began
to rise out of silence & reflexiveness, just
as if with a mind of their own so too do rise
their middle fingers as they pass each other
in the hallway. His middle-aged reflexes
responded to the doctor's hammer
much in the same way as a 50-pound
bag of powdered cement sits out in the rain
beside the wheelbarrow & white chickens.
Cement is an ingredient in concrete much

in the same way cake layers are ingredients
in cake. He mowed his lawn much in the same
way his neighbor doesn't, which is to say
he mowed his lawn, picked his dandelions,
& showed consternation much in the same
way a seasoned art critic when asked by
a stranger on a plane, "Oh, can I show you
my portfolio because it contains a point
of view much in the same way no artist
ever has?" And so he undermined much
in the same way actual miners in an actual
mine under an actual lake mine. The salt
was salty much in the same way salt tends
to be. And he thusly therapied much in
the way his ancestors didn't. He drank
much the same way his parents didn't.
Which is to say, he forsook what he'd
been taught much in the same way
cults don't. And he caught in the rye
much in the way Holden couldn't just as
the plane landed on the runway much
in the way models don't. We then parked
on the driveway much in the way parkways
don't. And went on to Great in the Gatsby
much in the same way the working class
can't. I'm living in a fantasy much in the way
religion doesn't cause war. But we nonetheless
arose among the roses much in the way roses
rise. And Paris shone much in the way
Akron can't ever, & so we Gertruded
on the Seine much in the same way
the steins emptied. No. Wait. Strike that.
The river emptied into the beer stein
much in the same way Gertrude exuded
exactitude exactly as exactly attitude exactly
Gertrude, for after all, we couldn't stop in
the same way should became shouldn't,
would wouldn't, could couldn't, did didn't,
want wanted, meaning meant, the elusive
illuminated, & a wood chuck could chuck
wood. In this manner, forever & beyond
the end of the universe & through all things
indefinitely & infinitely, thought should
be discouraged because panic begets panic
begets the fact the panic sometimes cannot
be unpanicked simply by saying, "Don't."

Nuance Near Mount Rainier, Washington, 1947

For Kenneth Arnold & Carl Sagan

Yes, I understand *it flew like a saucer* sounds virtually
like *flying saucer,* but *it soared like a blimp* isn't like
soaring blimps, especially if the antecedent of *it* is *plane*
& thus it becomes *the plane flew like a blimp*
instead of *flying blimps*, & when in the hell
did all these blimps get here? Moths to flames,
guitar solos to Led Zeppelin. Running over the hills
& faraway isn't akin to hilly running in the same
way it grew like a weed is not the same as growing
weed or it sprouted like a bean is not the same
as sprouting beans because we all agree green beans
are overrated, even if they are one of the three sisters,
because becaused like a because isn't necessarily one
of the best clauses, nor one of the wonderful things
he does because because because because of its
antecedent antecedented just all screwed up,
just as concrete is not the same as concreting
antecedents. And now we've a nice foundation
to build upon. Kenneth Arnold told one newsman
that it *flew like a saucer,* but never actually said it was
a flying saucer, & there were nine of them, not one,
& if aliens have been visiting us for the duration
of the planet's existence, why then did alien sightings
only begin after 1947, when flying saucers first flew
near Mount Rainier & up until that point in time
all those little green men were mostly a version
of The Blessed Virgin Mary herself—sign-of-the-cross—
or some fire-breathing-floating-invisible-incorporeal
dragon in my garage hoax because you can't disprove
that I have a fire-breathing-floating-invisible-incorporeal
dragon in my garage. Headless horseman not unlike
horsing headless, but a telltale heart is not equal to
a heartening tale. You'd think apparitions & visitations
would at least have the decency to visit a mammal
with more institutional memory than we possess.
Because who's going to believe this with their own
eyes as wide as aliens, even if we've never eyed
aliens, the apostles never apostatized, or blanked
it like a blank, not blanking blank? The absence
of evidence isn't evidence of absence, the cause
of effect isn't always the effect of a cause, &

being bamboozled once or for years doesn't
equate to a perpetually bamboozled being,
so long as you don't waste that mistake.
This is to say, you may overestimate prayer's
power almost as much as you cede too much
power to one guy, deifying a demagogue who's
actually, actively bamboozling your deity's belief
system. Thus, it looks like I'm going to hell
is not the same as hellish looks. Kenneth Arnold
told one newsman that it *flew like a saucer*, but
never actually said it was a *flying saucer*, &
there were nine of them—blimps not newsmen—
not one, & if they'd quoted him accurately,
how differently all those alien abduction stories
would have turned out, & maybe we'd still
be on about shrines, or some other self-fulfilling
prophesy wherein god didn't make man in
his image or garage but rather man made god
in his own image, somehow now white
& European, or some other form of weird
obsession involving abduction, sexual probing,
acceptance & abandonment, & shared public
vision like a virus like a very old man with
enormous wings, sunflowers not beans sprouting
from the leper's sores, & would you like to see
the fire-breathing-invisible-incorporeal dragon
in my garage? He's just floating like a saucer—
just over there, yep right over there—but he's
definitely not a flying saucer.

The Ambient Sounds of Assurance

I imagine picking up a seashell,
pressing the conch's heft against
my ear even though there's no real
beach near, but its coiled & empty
cavity seals with my canal & my
attention zoom-locks into focus
as I hear the hollow ocean woosh
with such intent that my eyes close,
everything else falls away, & even
the world stops spinning for one
two three. Then slap. Hands clap—
I startle-snap out of it, rotation
resumes, & back here back home
I actually hear, antennae attuned,
a crotchrocket unzipping across
the east-west interstate a mile south
of where I'm Midwest sitting on
my summer night garden patio
& the distant bike fades & slow-fast
buzzes like a mosquito bothering
my ear & the brick oven brick house
windows are still open & I don't
want the A/C on yet because
we've been waiting all year
to have a little climate sweat
on our forearms & its mechanics
ruin nature & her peripheral noises
& it's been night for a few hours
with only a few left & most are
asleep & finally everything's calm.
Everything is calm & there are
faint illegible words & music
coming from the garage speakers
& now playing is that song that
played all the time in college &
I danced & it wasn't awkward
& god if only all those people then
could know now how I appreciate
them even still, a record of my
memories only stored in my brain's
fading folds. All this technology
today & yet we-meaning-NASA
sent a bleeping record player into

space. Given, it was with a gold-cast-
not-vinyl-cut record, but still. So,
if you could have ninety minutes
of your life be represented, recorded,
& blasted out to space: songs,
chants, incantations, mourning
doves or puppy litter whimpers
or horses or whales or humid
summertime crickets, or that
barely perceptible background
hollow-bass moon hum, thrumming
deep in your chest, in your throat
like movie theater surround sound,
murmuring as it rises, crescendos
just behind the hulking alabaster
clouds impersonating sultry silent
airships, which hour & thirty minutes
would you record & send? From
blues-bending Blind Willie Johnson
to "Hey Jude" to *Peter Gabriel Plays*
Live to Rachmaninov 2 to *Nirvana*
Unplugged to wait. Just wait. Lemme
go first. Please let me go first: my
wife's laughter. No. Seriously. That's
it. That's all I'd send. Just Bridget's
lilting laughter in a modestly opaque
with Monet greens-blues-purples
blown glass apothecary bottle—
a neatly corked memory capsule
whose potent contents could be
easily dispensed in the tiniest of doses
so that it never actually ever runs out.

Cosmic Velocity

Here, we're all becoming librarians,
wanna-be Alexandria curators, & it's
not even like we keep it a secret
because this isn't a Bradbury novel.
Well, no secrets other than to ourselves,
as most times we don't recognize what
we don't recognize until we finally
recognize it, as when we don't realize
we're breathing until breathing heavily
or that we've been growing until Mom
comments on our spurt & its newfound
gravitational challenges. Ditto for
losing, remembering, learning. We—
now decades-in-an-instant lifetime later,
with our garage-made little lending
libraries on tilted-axis pressure treated
timbers sprouting on our chemically
green lawns throughout our blooming
communities: *Get a Book / Give a Book /
Be Kind.* We with our ten-inch book
stacks on our nightstands & end tables
& shelves where knickknacks used to be;
cookbooks filling that awkward space
between the coffee maker & kitchen wall;
a paper accordion of spines propped
between the living room buffet's crystal
bowls—mints in one on one end
& Sanibel Island seashells in the other.
And only the tabletop gets dusted.
That's why books smell, you know.
Yes, it's partly their organic wood
pulp decay, but also partly the dust
accumulation, which is mostly our own
sloughed skin cells & hair & clothing
fibers & dirt & dead bug bits. We're
all atomic dust, spinning on this rock
at 1,000 mph, Earth orbiting the sun
at 66,000 mph, sun orbiting within
our Milky Way at 552,000 mph,
& our flickering Milky Way—
in relation to the cosmic background
of other distant galaxies—spiraling
imperceptibly at 1.3 million mph.

And yet *you are here*, bold red arrow
pointing at the map: carefully sipping
your still-hot tea in your favorite chair.
Heirloom afghan draped across your
legs. Cat or dog asleep & squeezed
between your outer thigh & throw
pillow. From your book, you know
libraries protect memories, culture's
proof, & provide evidence of existence.
From your book, you look up. Over
the rim of your spectacles to better hear
each & every single spring raindrop
plunk onto the windowsill through
the water beaded window screen.
The slight breeze carrying the fragrance
not of kerosene as accelerant but instead
of hemlock & hyacinth & freshly tilled
earth. Maybe there's a quiet symphony
in the background, or maybe it's just
raindrops, gentle breathing, & the faint
trace of that original smoldering fire.

Go to Your Local Lumber Yard

And pick out a 2" x 4" that's 8 feet long,
standard size, & a piece of sandpaper,
any grit. With purchase, you get 1 free
cut, so find a Kyle in an apron & kindly
ask him to buzz it into a 2-foot length
& a 6-foot length, which should allow
your planks to fit in any car, & don't
worry, you're giving this tree a good
afterlife. In your unclean, relatively
dimly lit garage, place the 6-foot piece
on that dusty old kitchen table you've
been meaning to refinish, so the end
of the 2" x 4" hangs well off the table's
edge. Now sand the board's butt end.
For 15 seconds—just 15 seconds. Time
is relative, but stop. Just stop. That's
enough. Look at the ground. See that
sawdust puddle you just created?
That represents the length of time
human beings have been on this
planet. Still in your left hand remains
lumber, almost all 6 feet of it & that
represents how long the planet has
been here without you, me, all of us
ever. If you next grab a handsaw
& can eyeball it, cut off about 8 inches
of the remaining board. That's how
long clams—yes clams— have been
here, 8-inches, comparatively short
when compared to the remaining
5+ feet, but forever-long when compared
to the sawdust, & those clams might
be able to teach us something about—
because they're diligent stenographers—
geology & existence & meaning that daily
we only pretend to know, our 2 brain
halves limited by a single thick shell
whose lips can't be slightly parted
to filter only the wholesome nutrients.
Anchored to the reef, movement limited,
then shucked. Shell midden masquerading
as sacred cemeteries. Heaps of mental
muscles & molecular mollusks. Archeology
is a mix of garbology & speculation—yes

advanced study of garbage is actually
possible: as if we're all back in 7th grade
dissecting our first owl pellet, really digging
inside that ball, using the vole skeleton
& other compressed trash to make
broad inferences about an entire society
of owls. *Who who who.* Now imagine
fusing the 8 inches back onto the longer
2" x 4" & (re)attaching the sawdust now
sprinkled on your steel toes floating
above the pavement's inkblot oil stains.
You're again back to the original 6 feet
of iron-core existence. By chance, do you
still have, perhaps in the castoffs scraps
bin, that other piece of 2" x 4" just about
2 feet long? That 2 feet? That's how long
white-coated-pencil-pushing experts
expect this ball of dirt & metal & ocean
has left until this all goes kaput, until
our glowing orb of hydrogen & helium
fries what remains: roughly 1.5 billion
years. Do the math. 2 feet in the 1 hand.
Just shy of 6 feet in the other. Sandpaper
& saws. Bivalves. Instructional owl orbs
& deforestation & carbon footprints.
Garbage dumps as monuments to our
collectively discarded culture. And yet
there you are, trying to make sure the part
in your hair is just perfectly perfect,
maximum hold aerosol, trying too hard
to be the sharpest person in the room,
instead of just being a decent person
in the world. Worrying about everything
too far beyond your control, trying
so damn hard to be significant. Please
know this, & this is perhaps just 1 reason
for their modest 500-million-year endurance:
1 clam never turns & asks of another clam,
Does this outfit really look okay on me?
before walking to the car in the garage
for his long commute, loafer sole slipping
on the few particles of unswept sawdust
inexplicably still falling. Zipping through
shafts of light like tiny comets, streaking
& dusty flames hurtling toward impact,
bursting with meaning at the speed of light.

V.

Gunga. Gunga Ga Lunga.

When anthropologists find my bones
in 50,000 years in a cave in southern
France—because that's where all the
cool bones are discovered—I wonder if
my bones will be mixed with the now
100,000 year old antediluvian bones
of my ginger cousin species, Neanderthals,
which would explain my salt & paprika
complexion & complex lotion system
for dealing with the sky monster's ball of fire
radiating my un-deer-hide-covered skin
as I sipped accidentally fermented berries
by our pack's watering hole with Thag
who wouldn't stop one-finger scratching
his deeply ridged scalp. Will my mostly intact
skeleton be found among the other, artfully
composed skeletons in a semicircle around
our hearth—not really different from a fall
night's back patio firepit & raucous cocktails
with neighbors until Todd insists that it's
the last one because he has an early flight
to Baltimore? At that hearth epicenter, will they
find my metatarsals just so, arched, petrified,
resting on a rock just so, feet in that sweet spot
just between too hot & too chilly, ideal &
permanent primordial toastiness? What'll they
surmise when they find my tools, not too far
from my limestone recliner? A DeWalt 20-volt
Max XR Lithium Ion Brushless Drill that
was still useful once I killed the flashlight
& clearly had no plug to recharge the battery,
but monochromatic Thag still loved the bright
yellow & he was just the ape to use it to conk
a jackal or two on the noggin when the jackals
again got too close & clearly were asking

for a conking, we all nodded & grunted,
perhaps the first jury of his peers. Was our
group impressed with my three-inch pocketknife,
now well worn, but clearly it served its purpose
as a slicer, dicer, stabber, & you wouldn't believe
how much it saved our almost pristinely preserved
teeth, all that wooly mammoth carcass gnawing
because Jane wanted a new winter coat & Billy
finally came of age enough to carry a sharp
spear—such a thin line between tool & weapon.
That little knife led to my longwinded
& likely terribly incomplete lectures about
extracting metals from that mountain over yonder,
& we'd have to invent a sextant & compass
& keel to sail south across the Mediterranean,
raiding African rare element mines (without
the atrocity of colonialism) if we had any
hope of powering on this iPhone again.
"How far we've come, Thag, but we have
millennia to make up for," I open my palms
in my most courteous-nonthreatening-teacher manner,
straddling that thin line of explanation & being
condescending, "which means talking down to, Thag."
Well excuuuuuuuuuuuse me. No, Thag, I don't know
everything. In fact, the more I learn, the less I know.
But I do know that you & I won't invent
the printing press, electricity, the internal
combustion engine, flight, or mass shooters.
Goddamn. Wait until I tell you about school
shooters. We won't be the first or last with
hubris, privilege, imposter syndrome, anxiety,
depression, PTSD, hopelessness, bombasts
who teach with well-honed guilt & shame,
or an unwillingness to take a long, hard look at
our inhuman reflections in the tidal pool's stillness.
But I do know this: when they discover our
femurs & skulls, marrows & flints, they'll also
unearth our wall markings—clear evidence
that we did try to talk about those difficult
things none of us want to talk about—
if we can mention it, we can manage it—
& we did then genuinely try to take some
kind of responsibility, some kind of action,
leaving this great ball of dirt a little better off
than when we found it.

You Often Startle Awake at 3am Because Where Your Neanderthal Ancestors Lived in Caves It'd Be 9am & You'd Have Overslept Again & Everyone's Mad at You Again Because You Again Missed the Hunt or Gather

It's true. It's science. And science
is undefeated. Lemme amend that.
Science's winning percentage is more
like .500, as true science is proven wrong
as much as right, & to inflate its victories
or records would be anti-science hero
worship, & we certainly don't need any
more of that. *It ain't the way I wanted it.*
I can handle things! I'm smart! Not like
everybody says... like dumb... I'm smart
and I want respect! Listen, little buddy,
I know you're smart. Sure, you are.
But maybe ease up on the insistence
& go down to the watering hole &
catch us some fish for supper? Thanks.
Part of the reason we're so quick to
deify rock stars, politicos, celluloid
heroes, or pop culture influencers
is because in them we see that they
just might have broken the continuum
& actually have a chance at immortality
as their names might be remembered
longer than Neanderthals & we want
some of that glitter shedding off of them
like comet dust & if we just touch some
of that, we're soon enough flying &
Peter Pan, too. And if/when they crash
& burn, we just can't admit we were
wrong about them because then there's
no escaping the truth that eventually
we'll do the same, & then, for millennia,
we'll startle awake at 3am, reminding
ourselves how far we've come & just
how far we haven't.

In Lieu of Looking Toward the Ancients: Advice to My 12th Great-granddaughter

You'll be here—if my math, DNA,
& minorly-so-far-successful evolution
plans are correct—in about 400 years.
First, from what I've deduced, clean
water will be an issue, because it
always, even when silent or guttural
like language, was, is, has been, will be,
& well… consider staying in this Great
Lakes Region even if it's not quite
cosmopolitan enough for you,
as clean water is personal, social,
& political currency, & consider
the fact that there's always a downside
to everything, even when you can't first
see it, as when migrating birds couldn't
see the quiet swoosh clean power
windmills slow swirling outside
Magee Marsh & nighttime & well-
intentioned Subarued & Birkenstocked
conservationists couldn't have imagined
their numbers sliced into a percentage.
As when the desire to include still
excludes someone, inadvertently
& sorry but nonetheless. Next,
& this is important: newspapers.
They were really cool, if you can get
your hands on one, if temporary
& ink rubbing off silvery as your
window is open & it's spread out
before you on the floor & you're letting
it all in, springtime & a version of faith
derived from primeval symbols & those
sheets—thin almost translucent—were
both necessary for connecting us &
medieval Venetians and/or/also
walled barriers between you
& the other subway riders,
not unlike the social barriers of
the current smartphones that Guttenberg
& Babbage never could have imagined,
let alone properly cited the Roman
abacus, Hellenic star charts, or Persian

or Chinese cogs & wheels, simultaneous
independent invention, but without
the means to share, workshop, improve,
& yet still vital are Silly Putty attempts
to capture & laugh despite the bold
screaming headline font of yesterday's
terror, as if super thin trees, recast pulp,
could preserves some small proof
of *I was here* carved into the top
of a picnic table in the park. Trees.
Hopefully y'all have remembered
their relevance, even when we
didn't. Chinese Proverb: when is
the best time to plant a tree? 20
years ago. The second-best time
is now. Trees more of a bridge to
heaven than any of our mortal
& marbled cathedral attempts.
Remember that the things underfoot
are often as beautiful as those
at the horizon. Not just green,
white, & pink marble panels of
the 13th Century Florentine Duomo
but the basalt cobblestones your
loafers keep tripping on as you search
for your favorite dish among the
restaurant menus peppering
the narrow alleyways. *If you want me*
again look for me under your boot-soles.
There will always be things more
surprising than a road trip in a coming
of age novel that's driving away from
childhood & simultaneously toward it.
Choose experience over stuff, even
if it's the small impossible wish of
hearing Byron himself pronounce
Don Juan. How little we'll ever know.
How long does the dream have to last
before it's just life? Lastly, & this is
important, this is important, this is
important: when you find yourself
in a room where you're not comfortable
& no one seems to get you, find another
room. There are too many rooms &
there's too little time & so take a road

trip & make sure there's music. Music falls into the category of things that are vital even when others can't quite hear yours.

Distinction Without Difference

Or difference without distinction
because my optic nerve frequently
gets tripped up by linguistic sparring,
& for some reason we all tend
to think if we can see it, then
it must be true. If it's a black & white
photograph, it must be a memory.
But color is the collaboration
of the mind & the world, says
Cezanne. This is to say that without
language, the color seen is meaningless.
Or else, how do you tell teal from navy
from turquoise from cobalt from
midnight from Virgin Mary
aquamarine from Marco Polo
indigo from just feeling sad?
And the trumpet trumpets
some kind of blue. When he
unweaved the rainbow, Keats
thought Newton ruined forever
said rainbow for all of us, exploring
the science behind instead of just
beholding the beauty like the dumb
apes we are, gaping by the shopping
cart corral in the grocery store lot
as we fumble with the new pocket
phone-camera-rocket-launcher
with retina display to try to capture
the no-filter Cindy Lauper true colors
of the arcing ephemera after a soothing
spring rain. ROY G BIV. We often
make up our minds to see what
we want to see instead of seeing
what's actually to be seen. Percy
Shelley, fighting with his fellow
Romantic, instead thought rainbows
revealed one million colors, not
seven, & even if he was prone
to excessive exuberance, he could
also account for gradients beyond
just seven. Poets, like scientists,
can't be originalists. Comrades,
all constitutions are bound to morph.

But Newton said seven, & since
you're stuck on making color singular
again, or trying to shackle color
again—depending on your political
party—you yearn for halcyon days
when a rainbow only represented
one. But white isn't the absence of color
but is instead all-inclusive, you loud
& uninformed heathen. The more
uninformed, the louder, by the color
of it. Instead, try diving into the palette
of possibility, into the cosmos of small
details. In the painting of a color, titled
by the color, of that color among
gradients of that color, we exist.
Like oranges painted by a ginger,
then titled ORANGES, among persimmons
nectarines, & tangerines. A bowl of fruit
on the side table isn't as snack-worthy
as a ceramic blue bowl full of various
shades of orange jellybeans. Care
for some orange pop, Orange Crush?
I've got my spine, I've got my orange crush
(Collar me, don't collar me)
I've got my spine, I've got my orange crush
(We are agents of the free)
Still lives are never quite still.
Frank O'Hara could paint oranges,
title it SARDINES, & I'd love
the play of orange next to blue,
just as Van Gogh loved the laws
of complimentary colors & decided
to learn how to feel color differently.
Color & language don't hate.
People do. If they choose. Hate's a way
to look at colors—others—from an
uninformed place, an unexperienced
excuse for not learning. So, choose not
to lay one symbol on another symbol,
one color onto another, one lie to disguise
another lie. Can't we ever be more material
than metaphor? Darwin's theory doesn't
undermine the existence of god; it
undermines the godliness of man—
we—from our eyes, with their millions

& millions of rods & cones, to almost
every part comprising the colorful whole—
are products of processes of long-term
slow mutations, not specially, spiritually
ordained/created & charmed & finite
organisms. We're never as special
as we think we are. We are distinct,
different, & all slowly, constantly,
kaleidoscopically transforming.
Here, take a look. It's really beautiful.

Olfactory Ecology

If all things were turned to smoke,
the nostrils would distinguish them
(Heraclitus the Obscure, 525-475BC)

Did you know early cartographers had a great
sense of smell? From Mesopotamia to Ancient
Greece, indigenous Americas to the high seas:
evolutionarily, smell is/was GPS, & your app's
accuracy—*does it insist you drive into the lake*
instead of around it? Hike toward or away from
the bear?—depends on the size of your brain's
olfactory bulb & epithelial receptors, biology's
Bluetooth. Causation, correlation, & maybe
I'm drawing too many conclusions from too
few fragments, but that's what our species does,
isn't it? Having an incomplete story rarely stops
us from swallowing the whole apple, as when
you accidentally sit next to the unshowered guy
on the inbound train you consider flight,
fight, freeze, or appease, a public health anecdote,
or you enact bigotry, codify policy based on
I know a guy. But now, if you have a poor sense
of direction, I question your sense of smell as
you thrust the milk carton toward me, insisting
it's not spoiled. *Really?* I'll try it only if you can
tell me how to get back to the bucolic. Back to a time
when human beings were decent to other human
beings—*if ever*—whether or not they wore perfume,
too much or not enough. Old science said smells
themselves—*not necessarily organisms*—caused
sickness: cholera & diphtheria & typhus
from the stench, a miasma of disease, foggy
stink clouds misting sickness over the rolling
hills: Shiloh & Gettysburg fields piled with
parts & people, mules & horses, & brother
versus brother, which is why Whitman loved
lilac until every lilac he inhaled afterward
reminded him of those nurse tents & amputation
pits. This was pre-germ theory, pre-bacteria
comprehension, mind you. But post-Civil War
understanding evolved slowly, as any evolution
is wont to do. Maybe it's not that you don't believe
in it; it's that you don't understand it. Or want to

because that might require growth. It's true: trapped
in tenements trapped between the East River &
the Hudson—narrow roads carried faint traces
of where nature used to flow—curdled offal gutters.
And the public's noses finally rebelled, trusting their
own whiffs & homegrown smell maps more than
weird chemistry & newfangled public health
departments, so government sued government,
traded bayonets for subpoenas, & amateur smell
detectives clambered over docks & crates toward
the abattoirs, tanneries, candle & fertilizer plants,
emerging oil refineries & unchecked capitalism,
searching for a target for their anger, poor ventilation
problems needing a proper venting. Surely someone
was to blame. Almost always, someone is always
almost to blame, as torches & cigars, nosegays
& boutonnières, flowerboxes & flower beds,
camphor & eucalyptus, & potpourri-soaked
kerchiefs were only a fleeting fragrance façade.
Jacaranda & geraniums & sassafras & apple
blossoms. Hyacinths & aesthetics. Weird how
many 19th & early 20th Century novels barely
mentioned smell, perhaps because it was so
damn prevalent. Aroma a luxury for only
the privileged; stink for the rest of us. Heck,
even Coleridge gave Cologne a one-star
TripAdvisor review for its *two & seventy stenches.*
But sometimes, even now, we almost don't see
what's absolutely enveloping us, like citronella,
like the core of the Gilded Age: real gold often
obscured by the gold-plated & fool's gold,
which isn't weird because con artists have always
thrived in times of transition & quick change.
After all, the same year that gave us the first
stop signs & smoke detectors & Shredded
Wheat also gave us the Wounded Knee Massacre.
But now, as if swirling in a desert dust devil,
baking brownies whirlwind around us, braced
between the orange peel ceiling & honey maple
hardwoods, not just because the molecular scents
are so comforting, but because we know there's
a gooey-crunchy corner piece for us five minutes
after the oven door creaks closed. Care to keep
this chemical conversation going? *You may find
yourself living in a shotgun shack, & you may find*

yourself in another part of the world... & you may
ask yourself, "Well, how did I get here?" Maybe we
can't easily embrace the future until we've
taken responsibility for the past. So maybe
you find yourself standing in the July cornstalks.
And you decide there are too many caterpillars
on your ears, too many spoilt, so you turn to
the makeshift apothecary in your barn, mortar
& pestle a pinch of this with a dash of that.
Suddenly, you've poof-concocted a perfume
of moth pheromones to drive the male moths
crazy. Truly, to confuse them as to where their
mates might be, & so confused they are by your
magic potion, they don't mate, the ladies don't
lay larvae on your stalks, & *voila!* clean corn,
just by tickling & tricking the moths' proverbial
proboscises. Did you know the 11th century Chinese
had aroma clocks? Incense burned at different rates,
would indicate different times of day. So, 9am was
sandalwood, which slow-burned into vanilla, &
by noon, we were all smokey sage. The afternoon
brought on wisteria & lavender & alchemy, wafted
to Japan, & became juniper & pine, new mown hay,
myrrh, ambrosia, & nectar. And Roman theaters
two millennia ago would mist saffron wine among
the audience members. Smell-o-vision. Not unlike
the stage crafter trick of cleaning oversized mascot
costumes with bottom-shelf-gas-station vodka.
Orange blossoms. Rising petrichor & damp hemlocks.
Scratch & sniff. Delusions & infusions & absolutes.
Noses are just hosts for subatomic tape measures,
& dog feet smell like Fritos because of yeast,
bacterial olfaction. Not all noses know the tinny
pop, scrape, & waft of a new can of tennis balls.
According to Buzz & Neil the moon smells like
gunpowder, quashed campfire, both victory & death.
Napalm in the morning. And now all thrift shops
smell the same, no matter the Goodwill in no matter
the city: 18 malodor molecules; 12 from skin, sweat
& sebum, car exhaust & gasoline, dry cleaning
solvents, food particles & perfume. No burnt peat
from Ireland or old fat in the greasy garlic alleyways
of restaurant row, & folks with dementia often
lose smell, which is partly why they lose everything.
With fragmentary directions can we assemble

a purpose? Hygiene & hysteria & secretory cells.
You never cleaned out your lost lover's closet
because when you're super lonely you still hug
& cry into the hanger-hung shoulders of his old
flannels, his clove-musk a comforter & crippler,
& so, sinking to the floor, you try to recover
among his musty & well-worn leather shoes
& spilled cedar blocks. Recognition & memory.
Perception & pain. Beauty is emotion not reason,
which is why it's easy to recognize, more difficult
to describe, & not hard to damage. Objects,
including scents, are repositories of what we
can learn about people, even cultures. Creation
of perfume isn't a replication, but an interpretation,
& like any other creation, is about the process—
both the suggestions & the outcomes—as when
some European societies urged different perfumes
for different social classes. *Hello, sensory & social
inequity.* So we'd know them by whiff, which then,
of course, dissolved into segregation, as in centuries-
long claims by fascists that A, B, or C should be
blamed for all of society's ills because they
suggested that all ABC smelled of X, & next
thing, those inhumans were cast out out out—
exclusionary immigration bills & Jim Crow laws.
However, given our propensity to habituate our
noses—we can smell the cologne we spritz on in
the morning for about 20 minutes, but colleagues
will smell it all day—fascists often don't know
they smell like fascists. And their noses in each
other's asses are not unlike the ostrich's head
in the rotting sardine sand. Asparagus & patchouli.
The daily stench & simulacrum more evidence
that if you're not careful even the best science,
the very best sense experiences, from the olfactory
neurons to the visual markers & symbols, can be
polluted: it's not an amateur detective's jagged red
yarn line on a messy bulletin board; it's a straight,
thick neon highlighter to devolve from indigenous
mascots to Confederate flags to Third Reich banners.
Anise & durian. Black pepper & cabbage & tin cans
& pickles & formaldehyde. Urine & sulfur & bleach
& chlorine & mustard gas & Zyklon B—ultimate
devolution. So, wherever you find a quest for public
health, you'll find the public fighting that health.

Wherever you find attempts at greater good,
you'll find attempts to undermine that good.
Lemon & rosemary & spearmint & vigilance.
This isn't an invention. It's not rocket science.
It's human nature at its most unfortunate. And
at this point, you'd think we'd be able to smell
the difference. But time & again we forget that
if they grow in a healthy orchard, the end products
of apple trees aren't apples. They're more apple trees.

"We're Taught to Faun Over Authority and Turn Upon the Vulnerable Outside It"

Quoted from Christopher Hitchens' *Hitch-22* (2010)

There's an 89.4% chance that the place you slept
for your first 500 nights determine which god
you believe in. We're not talking Zeus, Bucko.
Though, if we're talking Mykonos 2500 years ago,
okay Zeus. And my buddy George once joked
he'd teach his kids the sun was, in fact, Apollo's
chariot wheel streaking across the sky. But raised
in a place that's like 90% Irish Catholic, a former
source of pride, I do wonder how close to Buddha
I'd be today if born at the base of a Far East
Mountain. Mountains sing, after all, & one
of the only facets of the Vatican I still appreciate
is the music, which still makes me feel closer
to the fantastic heaven even if heaven isn't
a thing anymore, but the feeling of hope still feels
most like awe when it's divorced from shame.
Shame is only one teaching method, but you
don't realize that until you realize that, but even
then it's best to keep your mouth shut, especially
if you live again inside the Venn diagram of where
belief overlaps family. So much emphasis on roots.
Perhaps not enough on branches. As when
a tree discovers she's meant to be a violin &
her notes, now liquid architecture, evaporate
like rainbow mist above the frozen forest
cathedral that was once her home. No greater
joy than realizing the "you are here" red pin
on the map can move just by wearing out
a library card. Look, likely, you really don't care
what I believe, nor I you, as we're not married
& don't pay each other's bills. I'm just saying
Earth is 4.5 billion years old, Homo sapiens maybe
350,000 years old, & the cognitive faculties
in the slab of meat above our shoulders only
kicked in 70,000 years ago. Then there's this dude
who walked Earth 2,000 years ago—that's like 60
seconds ago in evolutionary scale, & yeah
60 seconds ago, this dude enters the room
& starts sorting winners & losers, wings
& pitchforks, & within seconds this entire

institution erupts, codifies some great ideas,
but then spectacularly markets & bureaucratizes:
taxes, collects, hoards, colonizes, inquisitions,
demonizes, whitens & masculinizes, & yeah
that's a little bit presumptuous toward the billions
of folks outside of our little-oh-this-is-the-singular-
definite-point-of-view Venn circle. Maybe I'm
saying too much. But I beat myself up about
how often I've not spoken up, afraid of getting
beat up, how respect for authority is used as a ruler-
across-the-knuckles-encourager for not speaking
up. Politicos don't have a monopoly on fascism.
We're raised not to speak up to small injustices.
But small injustices accumulate. Fester. Exclude.
And treating people decently is a moral obligation,
no matter the god you believe in, if any at all—
morality doesn't need a deity. It only needs
imagination. And once you learn how,
reading up for others is a moral obligation,
not just a motto nailed to the building's ornate
architecture. In the end, thinking up might
end or make difficult other relationships,
but congratulations now you're an adult
& once you know/learn better, the responsibility
is there. And likely, any consequences of speaking
up wouldn't be as apocalyptic as you've conjured
in your mind anyway. Dinosaurs never tried
to crucify other dinosaurs across the sea,
contentedly smoking their cigarettes
a continent away, as if in a *Far Side* comic.
We needn't seek or encourage or inflict
extinction. It'll find us because we're living
inside an explosion. So, yeah. Extinction
will find us. Naturally. And it'll be okay.
Really. It'll be okay.

The Compass Rose is a Liar

For Two Heliocentrists: Aristarchus of Samos & Carl Sagan of Cosmos

In development are groundbreaking earbuds
which won't only instantly translate a foreign
language to an understood one, but they'll also
tell you what the speaker meant, as the new
proprietary physics recognition software accounts
for ambient noises, crests & troughs, doppler shifts
& pitches, frequency & tones, & I don't care
for the tone you're taking, Mister. The difference
between someone who always says what she
thinks & someone who can't ever say everything
he's thinking. Either way, someone's feelings
are hurt. *No offense intended* is never an excuse
for offense executed. And so, the big question
I awoke with, rattling around in my bell jar:
because magnetic poles are such an earthly
station, how are we supposed to determine
north versus south, east versus west in space?
Do astronauts never know which end is up?
Ass. Teakettle. And historically whomever
we place at the center of our map highlights
how ethnocentric we're capable of being,
even if it's the time spent thinking about
& acting for your rose that makes your rose
so important. Is as important as is important is
as a rose is a rose is important is as important.
And so & so, even directions can be complete
fabrications that don't mean anything beyond
our little earthly bubble. Or is our little bubble
all that matters? Our blue-green globe under
a glass cloche, as if an attentive gardener can
protect it from frost or horticultural annihilation?
Echo chamber inside echo chamber. Because
the sun rises in the east, some pious mapmakers
& prewriting pagans used to put her atop
the map, replacing my current Lake Erie north.
Or if in Chicago, *Where's the lake? Okay that's east;*
let's go from there. So I'm standing on the corner
of Rush & Ontario gesturing like a cartoonish
& spasmodic weathervane. *I swear she said*
the brunch place was this way. Until 11th Century
China discovered the magnetic north & clockworked

compasses, we could orient however we wanted,
as in that particular shrine or holy land should be
on top. Britain, Britain. Absalom, Absalom. Jerusalem,
Jerusalem. Cleveland, Cleveland. Did you know
Earth is about a marathon shorter than it is wide?
A third of us could run that distance. Equatorial
bulge. Just like middle aged dads desperately
clinging to rapidly fading youth. There's nothing
more certain than someone dumb & motivated,
a little bit of knowledge converting into galactic
confidence. But hey, at least I don't suffer from
tobacco-chewing-gun-toting-mediocre-white-
dude-small-penis-anger syndrome like the newt-
like hosts of a certain news network, & yes,
I mean news in the most liberal sense of the world.
I mean word. Topsy-turvy. Ringmasters & spectacle
creators & masterful marketers. I believe in fear's
ability to require the surrender of power & money.
I believe in pinwheels of matter, in the giant ball
of hydrogen & helium & fire & flares. Elevation
instead of a slow leak. Just what is the cosmic
speed limit in this town, anyway? And why did
newspapers—those oversized inky unfoldables
people used to ignore their neighbors & loved
ones behind, whether in their chair at home next
to a whiskey, or on subways, even leaning against
a lamppost, pretending not to be a private eye
eyeballing a possible perp—why did newspapers
always favor an astrology section next to the
Marmaduke panels instead of an astronomy
factsheet next to B.C.? And what happens if
time does slow down to the point where it's
moving backwards, like my running lately,
to the point where I feel like I can't gain ground,
where causality inverts & my footfalls hit
the sidewalk & then I lace-up my shoes,
where the ripples on the pond are followed
by a stone breaking the surface, & the torch
bursts into flame & then I light it. If I go so
far back I bump into a previous version of myself,
I'd give him zero advice because whatever I told
him he'd not understand until he was old enough
to understand. Apparently, with this imprecise
data, we need to be patient. To wait for a time
when better observations are available & more

accurate answers can be determined. As when
the Earth was no longer the center of the universe
& we realized that neither we nor the planets
deserve the privileged position we possess,
& even though gravity is an opportunist,
we needn't be.

When Dad Asked Why I Don't Go to Church Anymore

At first, I replied to his question
with a question, something I hate
& which isn't necessarily mature,
& could be read as bad faith
or avoidance, but I asked anyway:
Why don't you instead come run
with me Sunday for 2-3 hours
as the sun lifts over the Metroparks'
shale cliffs & red-winged blackbirds
pose on the dew on the cattails
in the wetlands & everything
from forearms to sycamores
to wildflower sprigs shimmer
with possibility, if only for that
morning until the next morning?
That'd kill me, he responded.
Konk-a-ree konk-a-ree, footfall
footfall footfall. Your sense
of peace isn't my sense of peace,
& even George Washington
stopped going. First, he stopped
taking the sacrament by scooting
out after the sermon but before
the eucharist, & then once
confronted by the pastor,
he stopped attending altogether.
He worked every day not to abide
hypocrisy, even if his teeth were
fake-in-a-way-but-not-wooden-
&-likely-from-another-human.
Giant asterisk for the slave owner
chewing with slave teeth. What
we don't always remember is
that history is reliant on memory
& if our memory is selective
then our history is incomplete,
& art doesn't stop being art
just because it moves underground.
But there, underground, we risk
not being us. Hiding. Is preservation
ever too selfish? When, in fact, that's
how most culture survived & revived
after all those raids & all those bombs,

no-matter-where & no-matter-when.
Underground. Like the past & present
residents of Kyiv, whose knack for
preserving language & culture is
a masterclass, given their history
of takeover: Ottomans to Romans,
Russians to Mongolians to Poles,
Austro-Hungarians to Lithuanians,
Soviets to Nazis, & back to Soviets
& Russians. Not to excuse the cruelty
inflicted. Never to excuse the cruelty
inflicted. And survival doesn't always
make one stronger. Often, it just
makes one traumatized. Persons
or nations. Uprooted. The hope
for better treatment because
Khrushchev was Ukraine-raised
turned out to be a delusion,
but it didn't stop hope. So if
we're not going to change,
or don't feel like we can change
others, we learn to fake what
we really believe. Fake, so we
pinch our thumb & index finger
together & slow motion drag
them across our pinched lips,
as if ChapStick, only permanent,
pretending to zip our lips closed,
& then twist an imaginary key
& toss it over our shoulder,
the burden too much to bear.
Our founders didn't want freedom
from religion as much as freedom
from *that particular* religion—
they worried about competing
sects getting too authoritarian,
using fanatical belief to bludgeon,
& burgeoning science didn't
look too shabby, but where
founders had immeasurable
underground battlefield skills,
their courage to resist Rome
or the local snitches, a la Galileo,
was a tad bit wanting. They were
more like Kepler, trying not to upset

the gods or his wrathful interpreters,
so they stuck with science & muted
versions of faith. Yes, absolutely—
you bet I'm judging past morality
based on current morality. Asterisk
because even back then, abolitionist
Tom Paine had conviction. Not-quite-
atheist John Adams had it, too. They
just thought keeping lips mostly
locked & putting it mostly in
writing instead was the best route
toward accomplishing the most
societal good, as, to most, perfection
has & always will be the enemy
of good enough. Look, it's not my
job to provide excuses for others,
no-matter-where & no-matter-when,
but founders, most folks, nor do I
have a desire for stake-burnings or
living out a castaway existence on
a newly-conquered-not-discovered
Bahamian atoll. Belonging is still
a form of breathing. The fact is,
their thinking developed. Take Lincoln
& some of his first ideas—thank god
he was a thinker under that stovepipe,
as he's proof we're not completely
judged by how we start but maybe
instead by how we finish, but yeah
initially he didn't think the freed
slaves should stay here, & the day
after 1862 Christmas he hung out
those 38 Dakota men in Minnesota,
bitter stiff wind blown east to west
across the leafless, hewn, upturned—
as if palms to heaven—& bleeding
boxelder gallows, poor imitations
of crosses. We needn't feel guilt
for ancestral sins. Unless we
choose to ignore those ancestral
sins. Mistakes are only wasted
if we choose to never learn nothing
from them. We needn't misrepresent
our cosmic origins, we needn't
be fooled into thinking we need

to serve an institution in order
to know ourselves, we needn't
be the cause or result of dangerous
repression, & we needn't fill
our lack of knowing with a well
of wishes. Because time is both
an emotion & a religion, I'm
working on becoming emotionally
agnostic because everything doesn't
need to be done-slash-known right
this very moment. Everything in
the past will eventually morph
into a kaleidoscope of what
will seem like just one moment,
a cubist rainbow rewoven from
seven back into a single color,
a single galactic brilliance,
& eventually we'll all be past tense,
but for now, in the slowing of this
globe—if I can just slow this globe
& this mind—it'll allow me to
breathe & enjoy the birdsongs
just a little bit more.

Everything We've Taken the Time to Learn, We'll Eventually Forget

The scientific theories, universal equations,
recipes, driving directions, sports statistics,
& I've never been good with names anyway.
The brand of chocolate you prefer, the exact
amount of feathery pressure you enjoy from
my body part to your body part. Or foreign
vocabulary hastily scribbled on now-well-worn
index cards, & dead white dudes who wrote
XYZ & in which order; geologic time stamps,
thousands of song lyrics & opening piano notes,
gods & generals & criminals & heroes,
as if any of us can be one-word defined. And
what're the names of that new young couple
who bought the Smith's house down the block?
The neighborhood's really turning over. And
"i" before "e" except after "c," birthdays
& anniversaries, & what you came into this
room in the first place for because your glasses
are atop your head & you're holding your
phone; no, I haven't seen your keys, but breathe,
& did you unplug the iron before you left?
Did you lock the back door? Why did you start
with him in the first place? Why you left.
Why you forgave. What you chose not to.
That the plot is one-part events, two-parts
the why they happened. Cynicism &
sarcasm & inside jokes & superstitions
& little stitions & Jeopardy categories
of all your so-called expert areas. All gone.
Gonzo. Sayonara. How to login, remember,
think, walk, act, lie, dream, distill water,
start a fire, fight germs, hide, hunt, eat, breathe.
Poof, like slowly, sweetly sifted powdered
sugar atop Grandma's Famous French Toast.
In neat little dust piles congealed in butter pools.
As if dry yet misty fallen constellations. Star
charts of everything you once knew that no
member of any genus or species will ever
remember exactly as you did. If you're lucky,
those preserved ashy clumps will remain
on the floor of the satin-lined box in the dirt
near the crabapple with the pair of Northern
Cardinals over on the back hill of the cemetery

boundary, & after your last grandkid kicks,
no one will ever visit again, grave marker
or not. Yes, in less than 26,000 days—
25,000, 24,000, 23,000, 22, 21, 20, 19—
tick tick tick—you'll have no more days.
And likely 75 years after that, no one will
remember your days or name or the small
philosophical wars your privilege allows
you to wage, like your irritation at your
species' inability to park neatly between
the lines in the grocery store lot. But this
doesn't mean you don't allow yourself
to wonder. To wonder & to soak up
wonder, those little moments that leave
your jaw hanging slack like some dumb
ape because suddenly you almost can't
stand the beauty from thank-god-another
sunrise. This is going to be a good day.
You'll make present tense present. You'll
slow down. For now, you'll slow down &
stay right here because the meaning is inside
the process. It always has been.

NOTES & ACKNOWLEDGMENTS FOR *AND & AND*

I.

Part of a Traveling Exhibition

+ Previously published as *Narrative Magazine's* "Poem of the Week," Winter 2019/2020.
+ Inspired by Samuel Taylor Coleridge's "Kubla Kahn" (1797).

Briquette

+ Previously published in *The American Poetry Review,* Volume 28/Number 1, January/February 1999.
+Inspired by *Strike Anywhere* by Dean Young (1995) & "Personism" by Frank O'Hara (1959).

The Birds Know Why

+ Previously published in *Spare Parts Literary Magazine,* February 2023.
+ Inspired by *The Bird Way: A New Look at How Birds Talk, Work, Play, Parent, and Think* by Jennifer Ackerman (2020), *The Genius of Birds* by Jennifer Ackerman (2015), "Free Union" by Andre Breton (1921), "Round Here" by Counting Crows (1993), "Ornithology" by Charlie Parker, *The Road & The Passenger* by Cormac McCarthy (2006 & 2022), *Nighthawks* by Edward Hopper (1942), *Death of a Salesman* by Arthur Miller (1949), *Buried Child & True West* by Sam Shepard (1978 & 1980), & "The Red Wheelbarrow" by William Carlos Williams (1923).

Upon Seeing a Red-Headed Ground Beetle I've Decided: I'm More About *Protection of the Weak* Than I Am *Survival of the Fittest*

+ Previously published on *A Poetic Inventory of the Cuyahoga Valley National Park,* September 2021.
+ Inspired by *On the Origin of Species by Means of Natural Selection, or the Preservation of Favoured Races in the Struggle for Life* by Charles Darwin (1859), "Asking for a Friend" by *Radiolab* (2019), *Thinking Small: The Long, Strange Trip of the Volkswagen Beetle* by Andrea Hiott (2012), "Ironic" by Alanis Morissette (1996), "This is Just to Say" by William Carlos Williams (1934), *Outliers: The Story of Success* by Malcolm Gladwell (2018), & "Let It Be" by the Beetles (1970).

At What Point Does a Superpower Become a Burden?

+ Previously published in *Allium, A Journal of Poetry & Prose,* fall 2021.

Sometimes I Worry That My Imposter Syndrome Isn't Good Enough Imposter Syndrome

+ Previously published in *The Viridian Door,* Issue 2, February 2023.

A Review of *History of the Rain* by Niall Williams

+ Previously published in *Curio Cabinet Magazine,* Issue II, May 10, 2023.
+ Inspired by *History of the Rain* by Niall Williams (2014).

Meme Machine: */noun/* Nothing More Than Cogs & Gears That Produce Cultural Replications, Fanciful Flights, & Losing Battles for Long-Term Evolution, Unless You End Up Under Glass in the Natural History Museum

+ Previously published in *The Dillydoun Review,* August 2022.
+ Inspired by *The Catcher in the Rye* by J.D. Salinger (1951), "Lying in a Hammock…" by James Wright (1961), *Uncle Vanya* by Anton Chekhov (1898), *Unweaving the Rainbow* by Richard Dawkins (1998), *Finding Nemo* (2003), *& The Clockwork Universe: Isaac Newton, the Royal Society, and the Birth of the Modern World* by Edward Dolnick (2011).

Today Reminds Me
+ Previously published in *Allium, A Journal of Poetry & Prose,* fall 2021.
+ Inspired by *Permanent Record* by Edward Snowden (2019).

II.

The Cosmos of Small Details: When A Young Poet Asked for Advice
+ Previously published in *Ink Sweat & Tears,* November 2022.
+ Inspired by *The Magic of Reality: How We Know What's Really True* by Richard Dawkins (2011), *The Hitch-Hiker's Guide to the Galaxy* by Douglas Adams (1979), *& Lyrical Ballads, with a Few Other Poems* by William Wordsworth and Samuel Taylor Coleridge (1798, 1805).

Dear Sadness,
+ Previously published in *The Parliament Literary Journal,* Mortality Issue, June 11, 2023.
+ Inspired by *Bittersweet: How Sorrow and Longing Make Us Whole* by Susan Cain (2022), *The Cellist of Sarajevo* by Steven Galloway (2008), "Miss Sarajevo" by U2 (1995), *Gone: A Girl, a Violin, a Life Unstrung* by Min Kym (2017), & "Like a Scarf" by James Tate (1994).

Arithmetic Word Problem: On Turning Fifty
+ Previously published in *Spare Parts Literary Magazine,* February 2023.

A History of the People Who've Shaped Me, Even When They Weren't Trying to Shape Me
+ Previously published in *Bullshit Lit,* April 14, 2023.
+ Inspired by *The Lincoln Highway* by Amor Towles (2021) & *The Golden Spruce: A True Story of Myth, Madness, and Greed* by John Valliant (2013).

Willy Loman Syndrome
+ Inspired by *Death of a Salesman* by Arthur Miller (1949).

My Superpower is Waking Up at 3am & Not Falling Asleep No Matter What I Do
+ Previously published in *Bullshit Lit,* April 14, 2023.
+ Inspired by *The Tiger: A True Story of Vengeance and Survival* by John Vaillant (2010).

Empathy Hotel
+ Inspired by *How High We Go in the Dark* by Sequoia Nagamatsu (2022), *The Scream* by Edvard Munch (1893), "Poem" by Man Ray (1924), *Infamy: The Shocking Story of the Japanese American Internment in World War II* by Richard Reeves (2015), *Kafka on the Shore* by Haruki Murakami (2002), & "The Hollow Men" by T.S. Eliot (1925).

Prolific Ghost Fuel
+ Previously published in *The Parliament Literary Journal,* Mortality Issue, June 11, 2023.
+ Inspired by *Kill Bill: Volume 2* (2004), *The Remains of the Day* by Kazuo Ishiguro (1989), "Every Teardrop is a Waterfall" by Coldplay (2011), *Keats: A Brief Life in Nine Poems and One Epitaph* by Lucasta Miller (2021), & *Consider This: Moments in My Writing Life after Which Everything Was Different* by Chuck Palahniuk (2020).

III.

If the Water Molecules Making Up X Change Moment-by-Moment, Then the Banks & Locale Surely Define a River, Right?
+ Previously published in *Unlikely Stories Mark V,* August 2022.
+ Inspired by Season 2, Episode 1, "A Good Walk Spoiled—Rich people and their addiction to

golf: a philosophical investigation" of Malcolm Gladwell's *Revisionist History* (2017).

How Little I Know Of How Things Really Work In Florence
+ Previously published in *The Purposeful Mayonnaise,* Volume 2.5, February 2023.
+ Inspired by *Austin Powers in Goldmember* (2002).

Wanna Know How Geography's Helped with Anxiety?
+ Previously published in *The Gorko Gazette*, May 13, 2023.

Nine Weeks In
+ Previously published in *The Spoon River Poetry Review,* Volume XXVIII, Number 2, summer/fall 2003.

Travel Tip #3: Antarctica & Growth
+ Previously published in *JAKE*, March 2023.

Home Improvement
+ Previously published in *The Gorko Gazette*, May 13, 2023.
+ Inspired by *Jurassic Park* (1993).

Even With Proof, Victorians Were Less Willing to Believe in Michael Faraday's Never-Heard-of-Before *Electromagnetic Field* Than They Were an Early Version of Ouija Boards
+ Inspired by *Faraday, Maxwell, and the Electromagnetic Field: How Two Men Revolutionized Physics* by Nancy Forbes and Basil Mahon (2014).

When International Travel Makes You Feel Like You're a Time Traveler
+ Previously published in *Spare Parts Literary Magazine,* February 2023.

IV.
Travel Tip #42: For When You Stumble Upon a Time Machine
+Inspired by "Asking for a Friend" by *Radiolab* (2019) & "Ode on a Grecian Urn" by John Keats (1819).

Some Cultures Use the Same Word for *Blue & Green*
+ Previously published in *The Purposeful Mayonnaise*, Volume 2.5, February 2023.
+ Inspired by "Blue" by Anda Marcu, published in *Spare Parts Lit,* Volume 4, January 2023, *The Left Hand of Darkness* by Ursula K. Le Guin (1969), & "The Great Gazoo," *The Flintstones* (1965).

Meet & Greet with Zaphod Beeblebrox
+ Previously published in *JAKE*, March 2023.
+ Inspired by *The Hitch-Hiker's Guide to the Galaxy* by Douglas Adams (1979), *Pale Blue Dot* by Carl Sagan (1994), *Man's Search for Meaning* by Viktor Frankl (1946), & Brian Eno's BBC's 2015 John Peel Lecture.

"The Ships Hung in the Sky Much in the Same Way That Bricks Don't"
+ Previously published in *Red Ogre Review*, July 2022.
+ Inspired by *The Hitch-Hiker's Guide to the Galaxy* by Douglas Adams (1979).

Nuance Near Mount Rainier, Washington, 1947
+ Previously published in *Bullshit Lit,* April 14, 2023.
+ Inspired by *The Demon-Haunted World: Science as a Candle in the Dark* by Carl Sagan (1995),

"Over the Hills and Far Away" by Led Zeppelin (1973), & "A Very Old Man with Enormous Wings" by Gabriel García Márquez (1968).

The Ambient Sounds of Assurance
+ Previously published in *The Gorko Gazette*, September 2023.
+ Inspired by *Murmurs of Earth: The Voyager Interstellar Record* by Carl Sagan and Ann Druyan (1977), *The Interstellar Age: Inside the 40-Year Voyager Mission* by Jim Bell (2015), & "Fabliau of Florida" by Wallace Stevens (1923).

Cosmic Velocity
+ Forthcoming in *Moot Point Magazine.*
+ Inspired by *The Right Stuff* by Tom Wolfe (1979), *The Library Book* by Susan Orlean (2018), & *Fahrenheit 451* by Ray Bradbury (1953).

Go to Your Local Lumber Yard
+ Previously published in *Paddler Press: Peterborough Nogojiwanong's Poetry & Art Journal,* Volume 8, April 2023.
+ Inspired by *The Secret Life of Clams* by Anthony Fredericks (2014), *The Accidental Universe* by Alan Lightman (2014), *Einstein's Dice and Schrodinger's Cat* by Paul Halpern (2015), & "Vegetable Wisdom" by Mark Halliday (1992).

V.

Gunga. Gunga Ga Lunga.
+ Previously published in *Bullshit Lit*, April 14, 2023.
+ Inspired by *Caddyshack* (1980) & *Sapiens: A Brief History of Humankind* by Yuval Noah Harari (2017).

You Often Startle Awake at 3am Because Where Your Neanderthal Ancestors Lived in Caves It'd Be 9am & You'd Have Overslept Again & Everyone's Mad at You Again Because You Again Missed the Hunt or Gather
+ Previously published in *Crab Apple Literary*, Issue 1, Volume 2, May 20, 2023.
+ Inspired by *Kindred: Neanderthal Life. Love, Death, and Art* by Rebecca Wragg Sykes (2020), *The Godfather, Part II* (1974), & *Peter and Wendy* by J.M. Barrie (1911).

In Lieu of Looking Toward the Ancients: Advice to My 12th Great-granddaughter
+ Inspired by *Under a White Sky: The Nature of the Future* by Elizabeth Kolbert (2021) *The Sixth Extinction: An Unnatural History* by Elizabeth Kolbert (2014), *The Death and Life of the Great Lakes* by Dan Egan (2017), *A Season On The Wind: Inside the World of Spring Migration* by Kenn Kaufman (2019), "First Love" by Sharon Olds (1987), *The Overstory* by Richard Powers (2018), "Song of Myself" by Walt Whitman (1855), "Don Juan" by Lord Byron (1819), *An Abundance of Katherines* by John Green (2006), & *Paper Towns* by John Green (2008).

Distinction Without Difference
+ Previously published in *Emerge Literary Journal*, Issue 23, September 2022.
+ Inspired by *On Color* by David Scott Kastan and Stephen Farthing (2018), *Kind of Blue* by Miles Davis (1959), *Unweaving the Rainbow* by Richard Dawkins (1998), "True Colors" by Cindy Lauper (1986), "Orange Crush" by REM (1988), "Why I Am Not A Painter" by Frank O'Hara (1957), &*The Reluctant Mr. Darwin: An Intimate Portrait of Charles Darwin and the Making of His Theory of Evolution* by David Quamen (2007).

Olfactory Ecology
+ Previously published in *Alien Buddha Press Gets Rejected Anthology, Part II*, February 2023.
+ Inspired by Melanie A. Kiechle's *Smell Detectives: An Olfactory History of Nineteenth-Century Urban America* (2017), Matthew Cobb's *Smell: A Very Short Introduction* (2020), *Perfume: The Alchemy of Scent* by Jean-Claude Ellena (2017), *Smellosophy: What the Nose Tells the Mind* by A.S. Barwich (2020), *The Confidence Game: Why We Fall For it… Every Time* by Maria Konnikova (2016), "Cologne" by Samuel Taylor Coleridge (1828), "Thrift Store Smell: What Is It? Plus, Your Cleanspiracies" by *Every Little Thing* (2019), "Once in a Lifetime" by The Talking Heads (1981), & *Appleseed* by Matt Bell (2021).

"We're Taught to Faun Over Authority and Turn Upon the Vulnerable Outside It"
+ Previously published in *The Gorko Gazette*, September 2023.
+ Inspired by Christopher Hitchens' *Hitch-22* (2010), *Sapiens: A Brief History of Humankind* by Yuval Noah Harari (2017), & *The Far Side* by Gary Larson (1979-1995).

The Compass Rose is a Liar
+ Previously published in *Aôthen Magazine*, Issue 4, June 5, 2023.
+ Inspired by *Exploring and Mapmaking* by Dr. Ian Jackson (2006), *Cosmos* by Carl Sagan (1980), *The Little Prince* by Antoine de Saint-Exupéry (1943), & "Sacred Emily" by Gertrude Stein (1943).

When Dad Asked Why I Don't Go to Church Anymore
+ Previously published in *Unlikely Stories Mark V*, August 2022.
+ Inspired by *Arguably* by Christopher Hitchens (2011), *The Gates of Europe* by Serhii Plokhy (2015), *Bury My Heart at Wounded Knee: An Indian History of the American West* by Dee Brown (1970), *God is Not Great: How Religion Poisons Everything* by Christopher Hitchens (2007), & *Unweaving the Rainbow* by Richard Dawkins (1998).

Everything We've Taken the Time to Learn, We'll Eventually Forget
+ Previously published in *Muleskinner*, December 2021.

GRATITUDE

Bridget, you're most of my memories & all my best experiences. This is for you. Annie, Colette, & Izzy: may you someday know the joy & privilege of seeing those that you love the most set the world on fire. Keep doing it. Love you with all of me.

For your relentless support, thank you, Mom & Dad. Love you, Jeannie, Jeff, Liz, BK, TK, Rich, Tom, Michael, Maggie, Matthew, Lanie, Marin, Elise, Charlie, & Harrison.

Dean Young. Cor Cordium. You changed my life & never wanted credit or blame, but I do both, & you understand. The other great teacher of my life: Joe Toner. You were among the first to teach me to see differently. Thank you.

Chrissy Kolaya, Dobby Gibson, Scott Stubbs, James Bristol, Allison Intrieri, Mary O'Hara, Andrew Neltner, Michael Murray, Karri Offstein Rosenthal, Christine Sneed, Cameron Gearen, Philip Metres, Karen Heath, Vandana Khanna, & all the Ramblers & Hoosiers who've supported my work through the years, thank you.

Uncle Jim, I almost left grad school after my first semester. You talked me out of it. Thank you. [Go Irish GIF.] And Patty & Sheryl, your support from afar is appreciated. Thank you, Grandma & Grandpa Mac (I miss you both), Sue (Nora), Mary Beth & Dave (David, Annie, & Daniel), Bobby & Gina (Michael—miss you—Matthew, Shannon, Patrick, Bobby, & Meredith), Therese & Dave (Toph & Robbie), Cathy & Brad (Marguerite & Mary), Megan & Pat (Grace, Mary, & Danny). Pat & Jack Shannon; Debbie & Bruce (Cara & David), Trish & Ray (Eli, Zan, & Sam), Dan & Mary Pat (Kathy & Julia), Duffy &Terry (Katie, Lizzie, Danny, Grace, & Mary

Bridget), Megan & George (Anna, Jack, & Max); GPM & Rhonda, CV & the entire Victory family, Steve & Eileen, Jeff & Jo-Ann, Jeff & Dave, Linda & Jim, Melissa & Paul, Melissa & Dave, Erin & Melissa & Jon & Tom & Sean & Chris & Deanna & all my running friends & writing supporters: thank you. Slainte.

My thousands of students: I've learned more from you than I've ever taught. Listing all of you who've been so supportive of me beyond the classroom—classroom to friends to blazing rocket fuel—would be another book in itself, but I appreciate all of you. To some folks I've exchanged work with beyond the classroom—Taylor Zufall, Brian White, Sean Swogger, Charity Gingerich & Jennifer Betz—thank you.

To all the Golden Flashes who've supported my teaching career & played some part in the generation/support of these poems, thank you: Jessica Jones, Connie Kramer, Jayne Moneysmith, Leslie Heaphy, John Lovell, Kristi Yerian, Jay Sloan, Mary Rooks, Alexis Baker, Jim Seelye, Ann Martinez, Rob Sturr, Denise Seachrist, Chuck Baker, Andrea Adolph, Carol Blundell, Maggie Anderson, Margaret Shaw, Alice Cone, & Charles Malone.

Loyola University Chicago, Indiana University, & Kent State University: thank you.

Finishing Line Press (Leah Maines, Kevin Maines, Christen Kincaid, & Mimi David): thank you.

Megan Frankenfield: thank you for *Sultry Cleveland Light* (2023, Mixed Media, 30" x 30"). I love your art & how you see the world.

Thank you to the Ohio Arts Council for its support in the creation of some of these poems through an Individual Artist Fellowship.

And to all the editors at the literary magazines where many of these poems first appeared: your support is deeply appreciated.

www.ingramcontent.com/pod-product-compliance
Lightning Source LLC
Chambersburg PA
CBHW020337170426
43200CB00006B/417

* 9 7 9 8 8 8 8 3 8 6 8 6 6 *